Provincial Geographies of India

GENERAL EDITOR

Sir T. H. HOLLAND, K.C.S.I., K.C.I.E., D.Sc., LL.D., F.R.S.

BURMA

T0364293

BURMA

BY

Sir HERBERT THIRKELL WHITE, K.C.I.E.

LATE OF THE BENGAL CIVIL SERVICE

Ornari res ipsa negat; contenta doceri

Cambridge
at the University Press
1923

CAMBRIDGE UNIVERSITY PRESS
Cambridge, New York, Melbourne, Madrid, Cape Town,
Singapore, São Paulo, Delhi, Tokyo, Mexico City

Cambridge University Press
The Edinburgh Building, Cambridge CB2 8RU, UK

Published in the United States of America by
Cambridge University Press, New York

www.cambridge.org
Information on this title: www.cambridge.org/9781107600676

First published 1923
First paperback edition 2011

A catalogue record for this publication is available from the British Library

ISBN 978-1-107-60067-6 Paperback

EDITOR'S PREFACE

WAR conditions and consequent war service are responsible for the interruption of this series of Provincial Geographies. Subsequent reforms in the political constitution of India necessitated further delay; but, whether the Government of Burma remains under the Governor-General of India or becomes answerable direct to the King-Emperor, the Province must necessarily remain a geographical and political, as it is a distinct ethnographical, unit—a Burmese nation.

For this, as for previous volumes of the same series, the author has been chosen because his long and intimate experience of the Province enables him to present in true perspective a thumb-nail sketch of the land and its people. In this respect there are two living authorities who stand in a class apart—Shwe Yoe (Sir George Scott), whose writings have brought to the West a humanitarian picture of the "Silken East," and the author of *A Civil Servant in Burma*, whose service of 33 years brought him into intimate touch with every phase of Burmese life and administration, from 1878, when the northern limit of British control was restricted to the Province of Pegu, through the third Burmese war of 1885, when King Thebaw's misrule of Upper Burma was abruptly terminated, and the subsequent years of pacification and economic development, till he retired as Lieutenant-Governor of the whole Province in 1910.

The Cambridge University Press is fortunate in finding Sir Herbert Thirkell White with the leisure to review from afar the land which he served with affection and recognized distinction.

T. H. HOLLAND.

November 22nd, 1922.

NOTE

Except where otherwise stated, rupees have been converted into sterling at the conventional rate of 1 R. = 2s.

In the transliteration of Burmese words, the Government system has been adopted. Every syllable is sounded. Consonants have the same value as in English: *gy* = *j*; *yw* = *yu*. The vowel sounds are:

a—generally as *a* in *pa*; but sometimes short as in *at*;
e—as *ey* in *grey*;
è—as *e* in *père*, without any sound of *r*;
i—as *ee* in *feet*;
y—as a vowel always short;
o or ô—always long as *oa* in *moan*;
u—as *oo* in *boot*;
ai—as *i* in *pike*;
au—as *ou* in *lout*;
aw—as *aw* in *maw*;
ei—as *a* in *maze*.

Some proper names, such as Rangoon, Toungoo, have acquired conventional spelling.

Special thanks are due to Dr E. H. Pascoe, Director of the Geological Survey, who has most kindly written the chapter on Geology and practically the whole of the chapter on Minerals, and has collected the illustrations thereto. I have also gratefully to acknowledge valuable help and advice from Sir Thomas Holland, Mr W. A. Hertz, Colonel G. H. Evans and Mr Taw Sein Ko. Most of the illustrations are from photographs by my lamented friends, the late Major J. W. Alves, I.A. and Mr Arthur Leeds, C.S. To other friends who have kindly contributed photographs my best thanks are tendered. By permission of His Majesty's Secretary of State for India, the General Map is reduced from the map attached to the General Administration Report of Burma.

H. T. W.

CONTENTS

LIST OF ILLUSTRATIONS AND MAPS

*This map is available for download from 9781107600676

CHAPTER I

GENERAL DESCRIPTION

THOUGH politically and administratively included in the Indian empire, Burma is definitely separated from India geographically and its people differ from the people of India in race, speech, religion and manners. It may almost be said to be a part of India merely by accident. Separated from the peninsula by the sea and by ranges of hills, it comprises a distinct nation.

The remotest province of the Indian Empire, lying between 9° 58' and 28° 30' N. lat. and 92° 11' and 101° 91' E. long., it comprises an area of 261,839 square miles, in extent exceeding either France or Germany and far surpassing any other Indian Province. Its extreme length is over 1200 miles; its utmost breadth 575 miles. The whole territory is distributed into Burma proper, 164,411; Shan States, 54,728; Chin Hills[1], 11,700; unadministered tracts (estimated), 31,700 square miles[2]. A convenient division, in daily use, is into Upper and Lower Burma. The latter embraces all the country annexed in 1826 and 1852, that is to say, the Arakan and Tenasserim and the Pegu (now the Pegu and Irrawaddy) Divisions, including the whole of the sea-coast. The rest of the Province, that part which up to 1885 constituted the Burmese kingdom, is known as Upper Burma.

Lying on the east of the Bay of Bengal, Burma stretches from the borders of Tibet, Assam, Manipur and Chittagong on the north and north-west to the frontier of Siam. Northward from Victoria Point, the south-eastern extremity, the

[1] The largest section of the Chin Hills has recently been constituted a district of the Sagaing Division; but they are sufficiently unlike other parts of Burma to justify separate classification.

[2] The unadministered area has lately been reduced.

eastern front marches successively with Siam, French Indo-China, China.

Boundaries. A small section of the boundary in the extreme south is the Pakchan river. North of this, hill and mountain ranges mark the eastern frontier except where the rivers Thaungyin, Salween and Mèkong are the dividing lines. With China, the boundary was partially laid down by a joint Commission between 1897 and 1900 and was demarcated by

Fig. 1. A Burmese holiday.

masonry pillars, some erected in later years, as far north as the head waters of the Akyang river in about 27° 30′ N. The northern part of this boundary follows successively the Irrawaddy-Shweli and Irrawaddy-Salween watersheds. The extremity of the eastern boundary and the northern frontier facing Tibet, as yet undefined, are marked by lofty mountain ranges. On the west, other mountain chains separate Burma from Assam, Manipur and Chittagong as far as the estuary of the Naaf. Thence, west and south, to Victoria Point, the limit is the coast-line washed by the waters of the Bay of Bengal, the Gulf of Martaban and the Indian Ocean.

Geographically, without regard to administrative distribution, the Province may be regarded as consisting of five main divisions:

(1) Central Burma, extending from the sea to Tibet;
(2) Tenasserim, exclusive of the western part of Toungoo but including Karenni;
(3) Arakan, omitting the northern Hill District;
(4) The Chin Hills, with Northern Arakan;
(5) The Shan country.

Central Burma. (1) Central Burma lies between the Arakan Yoma[1], the Chin Hills, Manipur and Assam on the west, and the Sittang river, the Shan States, and China on the east. It is traversed throughout by the Irrawaddy river, partially in the north by the Chindwin. It may be sub-divided into the wet zone, the dry zone, and hill country. It must not be supposed that these divisions are marked distinctly like the squares on a chess board, but roughly the distribution is sufficiently accurate.

In the south lies the **Delta** of the Irrawaddy and the wide-stretching deltaic districts of Hanthawaddy, Insein, Pegu and Tharrawaddy. This vast expanse of country is a great alluvial plain. The true Delta includes all the districts of the Irrawaddy division, Bassein, Pyapôn, Ma-u-bin, Myaungmya, Henzada, a flat country intersected by countless rivers and creeks[2]. On the sea board and along the banks of streams and creeks are masses of mangrove and *dani* palm forest, tidal and swamp vegetation, elephant grass and savannah. In parts, as on the shore of Bassein, the coast consists of a gently shelving sandy beach but westward towards Cape Negrais, the one well-defined promontory, it is rocky and difficult to approach. Except in the north-west of Bassein and towards the head of the

---

[1] Yoma, hill ranges, in Pegu and Arakan, literally back-bone.

[2] A creek is not a small estuary but a stream, uniting larger branches, not in itself part of a main river. The word is in daily use but not easy to define.

Delta in Henzada, where bordering on the Arakan Yoma is a hilly tract, there is no high land in all this wide expanse. But here and there crop up narrow strips of dry sandy soil

Fig. 2. At the village tank.

from four to ten feet above the level of the plain, called *kôndan*, supposed to be remnants of old sea-beaches. A great part of the Delta is flooded in the rains and is unculturable. But here is some of the richest rice land, much of it reclaimed and protected by embankments. The general aspect, in the rainy season, of Myaungmya, a typical Delta district, has been thus described by Mr S. Grantham in the *Settlement Report*[1], published in 1921:

Along the edges of streams in the tidal area there is often a fringe of mangrove vegetation in which the *kyi* (*Barringtonia*) is plentiful and the *lamu* tree (*Sonneratia acida*) is prominent by its long arms stretched out over the water and occasionally

Fig. 3. Evening on the Irrawaddy.

obstructing the narrower passages and by its numerous round breathing spires standing out of the mud between tide-levels. Through occasional gaps in this screen the passenger along the river in July spies what appears to be a second river flowing behind a screen of jungle which grows up on a narrow wall of tidal mud; but later in the rains the second river is seen to be a continuous stretch of water covering the paddy[2] fields with the tips of the plants standing out above its surface. In places in which brackish or salt water arrives, intervals in the mangrove

[1] See p. 120.   [2] Paddy = rice.

screen are formed by dhani plantations, especially in the smaller creeks. In other places again, cultivation has been carried to the edge of the stream and the screen of mangroves is replaced by a narrow ridge on which grass or paddy is seen growing above the water. At neaptide, or later in the season when the paddy has grown tall, the edge of the land is more marked, but navigators are still glad to have posts and marks set up here and there to mark the course of the stream through what is apparently one great lake. The more northerly parts of the tidal

Fig. 4. Jungle folk.

area are now completely cultivated in wide continuous stretches of paddy fields, broken up by streams with a fringe of jungle along their banks but including no extensive uncultivated parts. Travelling towards the south, the colonization becomes steadily more recent, more and more uncultivated land is met until at length cultivation is in rare isolated patches among almost continuous *kanazo*[1] jungle. Everywhere then, the background

[1] "The *kanazo* is essentially a mangrove; although it attains the height of eighty to a hundred feet it stands upon soft tidal mud, supporting itself by wide-spreading roots, from which spring breathers which stand up above the surface of the ground and by means of their large stomata enable the roots to obtain the air which they require but could not get in the water-logged mud in which they grow."

of the landscape is a high wall of *kanazo* growing along the courses of small streams crossing the cultivated plains or forming one face of extensive patches of jungle in the less cultivated parts, and in the south reaching often to the mangrove strip on the water's edge. Even in the cultivated and cleared portions odd trees often still remain as reminders of the *kanazo* jungle which formerly covered the whole. The river bank, built up by silt, is generally the highest land, but the streams sway to this side and to that as they erode their beds, and the bends tend to move along the course according to the ordinary fashion of river-action; the high ridge is therefore missing in places, the middle levels being contiguous to the rivers. Here, if the stream is large, the paddy suffers from the waves continuously beating upon it, and along the main rivers a fringe of jungle has commonly been left to break the force of the waves and screen the cultivation behind. The cultivators' villages are squeezed into small areas of land, which is uncovered at neap tide and sometimes at all ebb tides, and in lucky cases land is found for the village which is hardly inundated at all; generally these sites are along the banks of the smaller streams, the force of waves on the main rivers being an objection to building there. But commonly in the rainy season, and in the case of a large number for the whole year, the cultivators live in isolated huts or in small groups of two or three houses out in the fields. The highest available land is chosen and its level raised by layers of earth, and on that the house is built; and the whole family group of wife and dogs, cattle and children are accommodated in the closest association. The man and his cattle go out to plough; but except for an occasional journey to buy something to vary a diet of fish-paste and rice the wife may not leave for months this small area of thirty or forty feet square in which the children too must build all their houses, wage all their wars and hold all their *pwès* and processions, romping with the dogs or dyeing the chickens in their leisure hours.

The whole of the Delta is infested with mosquitoes.

The people generally recognize different varieties of mosquito, but in some places the general view is that expressed by an old Karen, who assured [Mr Grantham] there was only one kind in his village, and on further enquiry with a view to identifying that kind explained that it was " the biting kind." In the south and west the sand fly adds his bite to the other terrors of the insect world, and some people compare these parts to Nga-yè (hell), saying that the water is all salt, the country is always submerged, and the mosquitoes and sand flies are the masters and asking what further misery could be devised besides this of revising the settlement.

Yet, improbable as it may seem, over some minds the Delta exercises a singular fascination. Straggling villages, pagodas, monasteries, at rare intervals, vary the monotony

Fig. 5. Village Monastery.

of the outlook. As one floats on a broad river or a winding creek with forest to the water's edge, at night with swarms of fireflies lighting the banks, many an aspect of calm and silent beauty is revealed.

East of the Delta are more vast stretches of rice-fields broken only by spurs of the Pegu Yoma in Hanthawaddy and Insein and by the Yoma itself which borders Tharrawaddy and traverses Pegu, clad with deciduous and evergreen forests.

The climate of all this country is hot and moist with a heavy rainfall. This is the busiest part of the Province with the ports of Rangoon and Bassein and other thriving towns. Negrais once regarded as a promising port has long been abandoned.

North of the Delta and deltaic plains lies the part of Toungoo west of the Sittang and the districts of Prome and

Fig. 6. Burmese family.

Thayetmyo approximately parallel with it. Toungoo is still in the wet zone, with rainfall heavy in the south and more than moderate in the north. Indeed, even the southern part of Yamèthin, the Pyinmana sub-division, adjacent to Toungoo, has fairly abundant rain. But Prome and Thayetmyo, on each side of the Irrawaddy, are distinctly hot and dry. In Prome and Toungoo are stretches of plain, as usual under rice cultivation. But a great part of these three districts consists of hilly country, spurs of the Arakan Yoma, the Pegu Yoma and its offshoots, and other less noticeable heights.

From the border of Thayetmyo up to about the latitude of the Third Defile[1] of the Irrawaddy extends the dry zone of Upper Burma. Between the Arakan Yoma and the Chin Hills on the west and the Shan Hills on the east, it includes the whole of the Magwe and Meiktila Divisions (with the exception of the Pyinmana sub-division), the Sagaing Division (except the Upper Chindwin district and the Chin Hills) and the districts of Mandalay and Shwebo. This tract includes wide areas of arid and sterile country sparsely covered with stunted vegetation, broad undulating table lands, rolling downs, barren plains cut up by many deep ravines, with frequent isolated hills rising abruptly from the plains. The Pegu Yoma begins in this area and runs through it from north to south. Elsewhere are other hill ranges. Pakôkku, Lower Chindwin, and parts of the Kyauksè and Mandalay districts are specially hilly country.

It must not be supposed that all this is a desert. Along the rivers are alluvial plains. In Minbu and Kyauksè a large irrigated area is under rice. Shwebo, formerly a dry plain, is now a flourishing rice district. The rice plain of Mandalay covers 700 square miles. On lands unsuitable for rice, products of dry cultivation, millet, sesamum, ground nuts, wheat, are largely grown. The hillsides are often covered with luxuriant forest growth. Sagaing is the only district altogether dry, without relief[2].

The great rivers Irrawaddy and Chindwin, and their numerous affluents, many of them mere beds of sand in the dry season, occasionally rushing torrents in the rains, as well as rivers of less volume in the east, traverse these dry districts. Meiktila is the only district in Burma, except Putao in the north, with no navigable stream.

---

[1] See p. 25.   [2] *Settlement Report*, Sagaing. B. W. Swithinbank.

In this tract are the city of Mandalay and the towns of Pakôkku and Myingyan. Here also are the famous oil wells of Yenangyaung. Of note for other reasons are the multitudinous pagodas of Pagan, most renowned in this land of Pagodas. Here the villages are more compact, each surrounded by a stout fence, sometimes of bamboo, sometimes of stiff cactus.

Though there are long dull stretches of river, with flat banks, there are also scenes of singular beauty. In the

Fig. 7. Deputy Commissioner's house, Putao.

midst, the conspicuous double peaks of Popa are picturesquely visible from the Irrawaddy for many miles. On the western and eastern borders the hills are marshalled in bold outline.

North of the dry zone lies a land of mountains and hills. Upper Chindwin on the west, with the Shan States of Hsawnghsup and Singaling Hkamti, bordering on the Chin Hills and Assam, bestriding the Chindwin river, is a mass of forest clad hills. Parallel with it, on either side of the Irrawaddy are Katha, Bhamo[1] and Myitkyina, with Putao

[1] By purists pronounced Bă-maw.

in the extreme north. The part of Katha which lies on the right bank of the river consists mostly of hills with intervening valleys, but about Wuntho and northward from Mo-hnyin are fertile plains. Three well-marked mountain ranges traverse it and there are abundant forests. East of the river are strips of plain country; in the basin of the Shweli, the Shan State of Möngmit; and some sixty miles inland among rugged mountains the world-renowned Ruby Mines. Save for level country on the edge of the river, and for the plain of Hkamti Lōng in Putao, the Kachin Hills compose the three northern districts on the borders of China and Tibet. Stupendous mountain peaks and magnificent alpine scenery are characteristic of this remote part of the province.

Tenasserim and Karenni. (2) On the east and south-east lies Tenasserim, added to the Empire after the First Burmese War, nearly a hundred years ago. South-east are the districts of Mergui and Tavoy, a narrow strip of plain land on the sea coast, backed by hills towards the Siamese border; for the most part rugged and mountainous, covered with dense forests. The mineral possibilities of this country are great but lack of communications retards their development. North of Tavoy, Amherst consists of forest-clad mountains with broad alluvial plains between the Taungnyo and Dawna ranges, watered by the Salween, Gyaing, Ataran and Thaungyin rivers. The wonderful scenery is pictured in Crawfurd's vivid sketch of the view from Martaban, opposite the port of Moulmein:

At sunset we reached Martaban, about twenty-seven miles from the mouth of the river (Salween). The prospect which opens itself upon the stranger here is probably one of the most beautiful and imposing that Oriental scenery can present[1]. The waters of three large rivers, the Salween, the Ataran, and the Gyain meet at this spot, and immediately proceed to the sea by two wide channels; so that, in fact, the openings of five distinct rivers, are, as it were, seen in one view, proceeding like

[1] Sir Richard Temple records a similar impression.

radii from a centre. The centre itself is a wide expanse of waters interspersed with numerous wooded islands. The surrounding country consists generally of woody hills, frequently crowned with white temples. In the distance are to be seen the high mountains of Zingai and in favourable weather the more distant and lofty ones which separate Martaban from the countries of Lao and Siam[1].

Moulmein, the headquarters of the Division, is one of the chief ports of the province. North of Amherst is Thatôn, a plain country intersected by ranges of hills and half covered by forests. Salween is a maze of mountains and woods, and so is Karenni, but with a well-watered plain in the north-west. The part of Toungoo, east of the Sittang, which completes this section, is also a hill tract.

Arakan. (3) The western part of Lower Burma is the Arakan Division including administratively the Hill District of northern Arakan which is geographically part

Fig. 8. Rustic bridge.

of the Chin Hills. The rest of the Division lies between the Arakan Yoma and the Bay of Bengal. Arakan was annexed at the same time as Tenasserim (1826). Bordering on Chittagong on the north, it has usually been more readily subject to Indian influence than other parts of the Province. Embracing the districts of Sandoway, Kyaukpyu and Akyab, the Division consists of a strip of level country along the coast, broadening out to a wide plain in the north. Spurs of the Yoma fill the inland area extending nearly to the sea in the two southern districts. In the south is a rock-bound shore; further north

[1] Crawfurd, 361.

the coast is indented by tidal creeks fringed by the ever-recurring mangrove and *dani* palm forests. North-east lies broken, hilly country, covered with dense woods. Kyaukpyu includes the large islands of Cheduba and Ramree. Akyab, the headquarters of the Division, is one of the principal ports of the Province with a magnificent harbour.

Chin Hills. (4) The Chin Hills include the district of that name in the Sagaing Division, the Pakôkku Chin Hills, and the Arakan Hill District, covering an area of some 12,000 square miles. This country occupies the western corner of Upper Burma, bounded on the north by Manipur, on the west by the Lushai Hills, on the south by Akyab, on the east by Upper Chindwin and Pakôkku. It is a mass of mountains intersected by deep valleys with no plain country whatever. In the Chin Hills district and the Pakôkku Hills, the ranges run from north to south, varying in height from 5000 to 9000 feet; the highest peak, Mt Victoria, in the Pakôkku Chin Hills, rises to 10,400 feet. In the Arakan Tracts, the hills do not average more than 3000 to 3500 feet in height. The whole Chin country is covered with dense forest, including pines and other trees of temperate climes, and in places glowing with masses of rhododendron. The savage mountaineers have been brought into subjection with much difficulty and are kept in order by military police posts. The headquarters are at Falam. Another principal post is Fort White, named after Sir George White, famous as the defender of Ladysmith.

The Shan States. (5) The great tract known as the Shan States extends along the eastern border of Upper Burma from 19° 20′ to 24° 9′ N. and from 96° 13′ to 101° 9′ E., covering an area of 54,728 square miles. It stretches eastward across the Salween as far as the Mèkong river to China, French Indo-China and Siam. In the north it marches with China; in the south with Lower Burma and Karenni. Its general aspect is that of a high plateau rising from 3000 to 4000 feet. The Myelat, bordering on the Meiktila Division, consists of rolling downs, with scanty growth of trees, intersected by ravines. East of the Myelat are hill ranges with intervening valleys; thence towards the Salween a wide well-wooded plateau, broken by isolated hills. East of the Salween is the great state of Kēngtūng and part of Manglün, the latter entirely hill country. Kēngtūng is broken and mountainous, divided unequally by the range which forms the watershed between the Salween and the Mèkong. Other trans-Salween areas are the mountainous country of Kokang and the territory of the Wa, a mere mass of hills. West of the Salween, in the north, is the extensive plateau of North and South Hsenwi and Hsipaw. Hsenwi is partly and Tawngpeng further north entirely hill country. The Salween runs through the Shan States from north to south and the Myitngè through the Northern States from east to west. Of the people, climate and administration, description is given elsewhere.

CHAPTER II

CLIMATE

As already indicated, a country of such diverse physical features and of such vast extent naturally presents a rich variety of climate. Rangoon and the maritime districts, as well as the plain country up to about the latitude of the northern limit of Henzada, are hot and moist. South of the southern edge of Henzada and Tharrawaddy, the Delta districts and the plains of the Pegu division have a mean annual rainfall of about 100 inches; fairly evenly distributed locally and remarkably consistent, the average being, however, substantially exceeded in Pegu and Hanthawaddy. The sea board districts of Arakan and Tenasserim[1] have torrential rains in even greater abundance. In the last four years[2], the annual average of these districts has exceeded 200 inches, Kyaukpyu alone falling a little short of that figure. The maximum average of those years was 253 inches in Akyab; the highest recorded rainfall in 1920 being at Palaw in Mergui, 279·17 inches. In this wet country, the rains, brought by the south-west monsoon, last approximately from May to October; they have never been known to fail to so dangerous a degree as to threaten the rice crop of Lower Burma. Welcomed at first as a relief after the steamy heat of May, the rains soon become monotonous. By the middle of August, with a rich growth of fungus on one's boots, one begins to tire of them. But it does not always rain day and night. On most days, either the morning or the evening is fine and gives opportunity for exercise. Cyclones are not very frequent visitors. In 1902, early in May, occurred one of great violence which, in Rangoon,

[1] Akyab, Kyaukpyu, Sandoway, Thatôn, Amherst, Tavoy and Mergui.

[2] 1917--20.

unroofed houses and magazines, swept boats high and dry, and blocked most of the roads in the Cantonment with torn branches of trees. Some years later a fierce cyclone ravaged Akyab.

This part of the Province enjoys no really cold season, but from November till the end of January there is a sensible fall of temperature, the thermometer descending

Fig. 9. Mandalay Hill, and water-lilies on the moat.

sometimes as low as 60° F. From February to May, the days are hot and oppressive, but the thermometer seldom rises above 100°. As a rule, the nights are not intolerably warm. In Rangoon, which may be regarded as typical, the average temperature, day and night, in January is nearly 77°, in May, 84°.

Further north, the climate changes gradually. Henzada, Tharrawaddy and Toungoo, approaching the dry zone, are almost level with rainfall of about 80 inches. Prome and Thayetmyo drop to not much over 40. These districts are extremely hot in the summer months and have a moderate cool season.

The real dry zone, from the old frontier of Upper Burma to about 60 miles north of Mandalay, has, for the most part, normally, an average annual rainfall of about 30 inches. But from year to year, it varies capriciously. In Pakôkku, the driest district, the yearly total is not much more than 20 inches. Though Shwebo has the highest mean with 38 inches, in 1920 the actual rainfall was under 24. In this tract, in the plains, the soil is dry and bare; in Spring and early Summer, the temperature rises to as high as 115°; and there is good and seasonable cold weather from November to March, the thermometer in the daytime falling to as low as 55°. At Mandalay, the annual rainfall is nearly 32 inches; the average temperature in January 70°, in May 80°. Scanty rainfall at times causes crops to fail on unirrigated lands and has, occasionally, produced conditions of scarcity approaching famine. Although the Summer is distinctly hot and parching there is no such fierce and fervent heat as in the plains of Upper India. The nights are nearly always bearable. And in Mandalay and Yamèthin and other places similarly situated, constant high winds, though tiringly monotonous, are yet welcome as tempering the excessive heat. In the hills of this area the extremes of temperature are 90° and 32°.

North of about the latitude of the Third Defile[1], the rainfall again becomes fairly abundant, rising from some 50 inches in Katha to 69 in Bhamo and 80 in Myitkyina, while the temperature, though hot in Summer, is cool and pleasant in the winter months. In the Kachin and Chin Hills, the heat is never excessive and at times the temperature is very low, the range being between 85° and 25°. In the high lands on the Chinese frontier, east of Bhamo, severe frosts prevail for several weeks, producing solid blocks of

[1] See p. 25.

ice to the astonishment of the Burman from the plains.
In the Chin Hills, the annual rainfall varies from 50 to 110
inches. The Shan plateau enjoys a temperate climate and
a consistent rainfall varying from 60 to 80 inches[1].

Hill Stations. In most parts of the Province, except the
true Delta and the plain country to the east thereof, are
to be found in the hills refuges from the severity of the

Fig. 10. Kalaw.

hot season. Maymyo, on the edge of the Northern Shan
States, though on a plateau only 3400 feet above the sea,
is yet comparatively cool in the warm months, cold but
not too cold in winter, wet but not too wet in the rains.
Kalaw, the Mussoorie of Burma, lying among pine-groves
on the border of the Myelat, is another popular summer
resort. Toungoo has a comfortable hill station at Thandaung and Bhamo the cool and healthy heights of Sinlum-

---

[1] A table of rainfall is given in Appendix I.

gaba. Mt Victoria and Kanpetlet in the Pakôkku Chin
Hills, ideal summer resorts, are inaccessible. But Popa in
Myingyan offers cool days and nights to dwellers in the
parched plains of the central dry zone. Even as far south
as Henzada, Allantaung, on a peak of the Arakan Yoma,
is cool and refreshing in the hot season. Jaded residents
of the Delta find here relief and recreation. A Commis-

Fig. 11. A wayside stall.

sioner's wife, Mrs Maxwell Laurie, has described Allantaung
in the columns of the *Indiaman*:

A few feet short of the top is a cleared plateau which forms
a spacious camping ground, shaded by great banyan trees. To
the West lies a country of broken mountains and steep valleys
straight across which from the sea comes a breeze, salt, strong,
invigorating. To the North and South across a deep, green
valley there is a splendid vision of mountains, stretching out
range behind range, beyond the limits of sight. Simply to let
the imagination roam along the lovely, sweeping ridges satisfied

and refreshed the soaring souls of persons accustomed to dwell on a deltaic swamp....Far away to the East lie the plains, and over them, shining in sunlight luminous in the last rays of evening, hangs the haze of an atmosphere almost solid with dust.

Burma is usually regarded as an unhealthy country. The mental picture is of a land of dismal swamps and deadly marshes, far different from the glowing reality. The impression of unhealthiness is due to the hardships and privations suffered by troops, police, and civil officers during and after the three Burmese Wars. In unsuitable conditions, much sickness and mortality were inevitable. But on the mind of the visitor in ordinary times, who lived in normal surroundings, the contrary impression was stamped. Writing in 1795, Symes says: "The climate of every part of the Burman Empire which I have visited bore testimony to its salubrity[1]." It is true that his range was limited to Rangoon and the country along the Irrawaddy as far north as Ava. But his record is of interest as indicating his experience in comparatively early times before the dawn of sanitation. On the whole, his impression was accurate. Parts of Burma, such as Northern Arakan, Salween, Katha, and all tracts lying at the foot of hills, are notoriously unhealthy owing to the prevalence of malarial fever. Cholera is never absent throughout a whole year, though serious epidemics are far less frequent than of yore. Plague has not been extirpated by the efforts of seventeen years. But cholera and plague are accidents. With the more rigorous application of improved sanitary methods, these diseases as well as malarial fever should be banished. Subject to these exceptions, the Province, as a whole, is not unhealthy. In particular, the swamps of the Delta and the great rice plains, though enervating, are not deadly. But it must be admitted that, everywhere, vitality once impaired is not readily restored. The annual mortality is

[1] Symes, 322.

about 25 per thousand. But the statistics are not entirely trustworthy. In 1918, owing to the epidemic of influenza, the death of nearly 40 per thousand was recorded.

Fig. 12. Burmese cemetery.

CHAPTER III

RIVERS

Irrawaddy. The dominant physical feature of Burma is the great river Irrawaddy, formed by the union of two sister streams. The actual source of the Irrawaddy was long regarded as almost the last unsolved geographical mystery. It has, however, been ascertained that the eastern and main branch, the 'Nmaikha[1] issues from the Laguela Glacier[2], in about 29° N. on the mountain range which separates Putao from Tibet; and traverses the Putao district, in its earliest stage, as the Tarôn stream. The western branch, the Malikha, rises in the hills surrounding the Hkamti-lông valley, in the Putao district. Both these streams flow southward till, some 30 miles above Myitkyina, boiling and surging over rugged rocks, they join at the Confluence. Above this point, neither of these rivers nor their affluents are navigable, being strewn with rocks, cataracts and rapids. The Kampang falls into the Tarôn with a sheer drop of 400 feet. From the Confluence, the united river pursues its majestic course to the sea for nearly a thousand miles. Above Myitkyina are rapids, mild and innocuous, easily navigated by rafts and shallow boats. Swift and clear as crystal, the Irrawaddy flows past Myitkyina, its course unimpeded till it reaches Sinbo. Between the rapids and Sinbo, the river is navigable by launches and light draught steamers throughout the year. Just below Sinbo, in the wet season, swollen by rains and melted snows, checked by a rampart of rocks, the stream

---

[1] *Kha*, Kachin for stream; *nan*, the Shan equivalent. Thus Tabak-Kha and Nan-tabet are the same stream and the same word, with Kachin tail and Shan head respectively. 'Nmaikha means "bad river"; the meaning of Malikha is not known.

[2] J. Bacot, *Le Tibet Révolté*.

Fig. 13. Adung Valley, head waters of the Irrawaddy.

banks up into a high wall of waters. Piercing this rampart, the Irrawaddy enters the First Defile, a gloomy, savage, rock-bound gorge, thirty-five miles in length. The Defile is narrow, tortuous, romantically beautiful, in places of unfathomed depth. Rocks in mid-stream, sudden abrupt curves, seething whirlpools, render navigation difficult and hazardous. In the dry season, with care but without insuperable risk, launches steam up and down the Defile, their movements strictly regulated, under statutory sanction, by the civil authorities at Bhamo in telegraphic communication with Sinbo. When the rains begin, the Defile, closed to steam traffic, is traversed constantly by timber rafts, sparingly by boats. Down stream, boats rush with more speed than safety. Up stream, the voyage is laboriously effected by towage from the bank. If the rope slips, the toil of days is lost in a few minutes. Emerging at Pashaw, named by an illustrious visitor[1] the Ruby Gate of the Irrawaddy, the river flows peaceably past Bhamo. A few miles below that town lies the Second Defile, not so strait and winding as the first but bound between beetling crags and set with dangerous eddies and whirlpools. Less sternly sombre than the upper gorge, it is perhaps even more picturesquely beautiful, with one most striking feature, the towering Elephant Rock crowned by a tiny golden pagoda. In spite of this narrow approach, steamers reach Bhamo at all times of the year.

From the Second Defile the river issues just above the charming village of Shwegu. Thence past Moda, Katha, Tagaung, site of an ancient capital, Thabeik-kyin, Kyauk-myaung, it flows placidly on to Mandalay. Near Thabeik-kyin, the port of the Ruby Mines, it is caught by the Third Defile, deep and somewhat narrow, but not to be compared with the Defiles above either in hazard or in beauty. A strong swimmer can cross from bank to bank. Leaving the wharves and the Hard of Mandalay thronged by

[1] Lord Kitchener.

steamers, launches and Burmese craft, the Irrawaddy glides past Ava, renowned in history, Sagaing, a typical Burmese town embosomed in tamarind groves, Myingyan, a busy port, Pakôkku, a trade centre near the mouth of the Chindwin river, Pagan, with its silent array of pagodas, Yenangyaung, redolent of earth-oil, Magwe, Minbu, the fort at Minhla, the old frontier pillars recalling memories of Dalhousie, the great Governor-General, Thayetmyo,

Fig. 14. On the Irrawaddy.

Prome, another ancient capital, the sculptured bank at Akauktaung, Myan-aung[1], Henzada, Danubyu, scene of fierce conflict in the First War, thence into the Delta where dividing into countless streams and creeks, it reaches the Bay of Bengal. One great offshoot above Henzada, on the right bank, forms the Ngawun, in its later course the

[1] "Myan-aung, a very ancient city, stretching two miles along the margin of the river;...a great variety of tall wide-spreading trees gave the place an air of venerable grandeur." Symes, 233. Written in 1795. Myan-aung has now sunk to insignificance.

Bassein river. Another main channel finds the sea at China Bakir, as the To or China Bakir. Other principal prongs of the Irrawaddy are the Pyawmalaw, the Shwelaung, later the Kyunpyat-that, the Yazudaing and the Kyaiklat or Pyapôn. The stream which reaches the sea as the Irrawaddy flows through Myaungmya till in its lower extremity it divides that district from Pyapôn. On the left, at Yandoon, the Panlang creek leaves the Irrawaddy and flows into the Rangoon river. Formerly navigable by steamers of some size, of late years this creek has silted up and is now hardly practicable except by boats. Below Bassein, the Rangoon creek, so called because it is the route for steamers to Rangoon, re-unites the Bassein river with the main stream. Similarly, below Rangoon is the Bassein or Thakutpin creek, the beginning of the water-way to Bassein, flowing from the Rangoon river into the Irrawaddy.

Before the making of railways, the Irrawaddy was the great commercial route from the sea to the heart of Burma. On the unnumbered creeks and streams of the Delta, as well as on the main river, were to be seen many a stately Burmese boat, often adorned with rich carving, propelled by long oars or wafted by brown sails as wind and tide ordained, with high stern where the helmsman sat aloft. Here, too, might be seen smaller boats carrying the peasant with his farm produce to market, a score of brightly clad laughing men, maids, and matrons to a pagoda festival, a dozen monks on some religious mission; and racing boats, long and shallow, with crews of twenty or thirty shouting paddlers. Most of these picturesque craft are softly and silently vanishing away. Multitudes of launches now make the sylvan creeks hideous with steam-whistles, the grinding of screws, the churning of paddles. The sampan, an ugly exotic, penetrates even to remote villages; and the graceful Burmese boats are being ousted from the carrying traffic by squat barges and squalid lighters.

The Irrawaddy is still a valuable alternative to land
routes. On the main stream, the bulk of the trade is in the
hands of the Irrawaddy Flotilla Company. Their steamers,
of shallow draught, run from Rangoon, through the Bassein
creek, past Thôngwa and Ma-u-bin, as far as Bhamo,
carrying passengers and cargo. The faster steamers run
single-handed, stopping only at important towns. Others,
known as cargo-steamers, have each a flat or barge attached
on either side. With them speed is not the object. Stopping
at every village and carrying on board a travelling bazaar

Fig. 15. Burmese girl.

or market, they present a microcosm of Burmese life in
many phases. Other steamer services ply in the Delta.
On the main river, steamers move only by day, anchoring
or tying up to the bank at night. Elsewhere they rush,
day and night, through labyrinthine creeks, often crashing
into the mangrove forests on the margin.

From the sea to Bhamo and two miles beyond, for a
distance of 689 miles, the Irrawaddy is navigable by
steamers at all times. But while in the rains it is a deep
and magnificent river, some two miles wide at Bhamo, in

the dry season its aspect changes. Then for a great part of its course, it is shallow, strewn with islands and with sandbanks which shift from year to year, impeding navigation and leaving riverine towns such as Bhamo and Myingyan often miles from the water's edge. At this season, only flat-bottomed vessels of very shallow draught can pick their way; sometimes even these are stranded. Often at Prome and below Mandalay, rows of steamers have been held fast for days. Elsewhere, steamers have grounded and remained high and dry for months till released by the rise of the river. Meanwhile the vessel becomes a stationary dwelling round which the caretaker plants a little garden for profit and for pastime. In the rains, high rises flood the banks to the destruction of growing crops. At the same time, the silt deposited enriches the soil.

The scenery of the Irrawaddy has been often celebrated. It is declared to be "as stately as it is beautiful; as passionate as it is serene." From the Confluence to the sea, it presents innumerable types of the picturesque, the rugged grandeur of the defiles, the smooth stream flowing between storied banks, the multitudinous mazes of the lower reaches. Sir Henry Yule, who accompanied Sir Arthur Phayre on his Mission to the Court of Ava in 1855 and who has recorded his observations in a classic work of absorbing interest, has drawn this brilliant picture of one gorgeous view:

The scene was one to be registered in the memory with some half dozen others which cannot be forgotten. Nothing on the Rhine could be compared to it. At the point where the temple stood, the Irrawaddy forms a great elbow, almost indeed a right angle, coming down to us from the North, but here diverted to the West. Northwards the wide river stretched, embracing innumerable islands, till seemingly hemmed in and lost among the mountains. Behind us, curving rapidly round the point on which we stood, it passed away to the Westward, and was lost in the blaze of a dazzling sunset. Northward ran

Fig. 16. View north of Sagaing.

the little barren, broken ridges of Sagaing, every point and spur of which was marked by some monastic building or pagoda. Nearly opposite to us lay Amarapoora, with just enough haze upon its temples and towers to lend them all the magic of an Italian city. A great bell-shaped spire, rising faintly white in the middle of the town, might well pass for a great Duomo. You could not discern that the domes and spires were all of dead heathen masses of brickwork and that the body of the city was bamboo and thatch. It might have been Venice, it looked so beautiful. Behind it rose range after range of mountains robed in blue enchantment. Between our station and the river was only a narrow strip of intense green foliage, mingled with white temples, spires, and cottage roofs. The great elbow of the river below us, mirroring the shadows of the wood on its banks, and the glowing clouds above, had been like a lake, were it not that the downward drift of the war-boats as they crossed and recrossed, marked so distinctly the rapidity of the kingly stream. The high bank of the river, opposite Sagaing eastward, was seen to be a long belt of island crowned with glorious foliage (and there are no trees like those of Burma); only here and there rose an unwooded crest, crowned with its Cybeleian coronet of towers. Behind this were numerous other wooded islands, or isolated villages, and temples, and monasteries, rising directly out of the flood waters. Southward, across the river, was the old city of Ava, now a thicket of tangled gardens and jungle, but marked by the remaining spires of temples. On this side lay Sagaing quite buried in tamarind trees.

Affluents of the Irrawaddy. Stated in order from the north, the principal tributaries of the Irrawaddy above Bhamo, on the left bank, are the Nantabet, formed by the junction of the Tabak and Paknoi, the Mole, and the Taiping. Of these, the Taiping which flows westward out of China is the only river of importance; the others are mountain streams winding through the Kachin Hills. On the right bank is the Mogaung or Namkawng which debouches at Sinbo, after passing Mogaung, the depot of the jadeite industry, and after receiving there, its main tributary, the Namyin from Katha. Below Bhamo, on the left bank, are the Sinkan and the Shweli, the latter a river of

some size rising in China; on the right bank, the Kauk-kwe,
Mosit and Meza, streams of no great volume or value.
Further south are the Madaya river known also as Chaung-
magyi or Nampi, which issues from the Northern Shan
States as the Mobye, above, and the Myitngè, Dôktawadi
or Namtu, below, Mandalay. The Myitngè, though its name
means "little river" as compared with the great river into

Fig. 17. Burmese boats.

which it merges, is of considerable size. It runs in a south-
westerly direction through the Shan States; is much used
as a floating stream for timber; and is distinguished by
the Namsan waterfalls of singular beauty[1]. The Myitngè
receives the waters of the Panlaung already joined by the
Samôn and of the Zawgyi, both from the south.

[1] These falls now provide power for electric works and their beauty
may be marred.

The Mu[1] river, pursuing a southerly course almost parallel with the Irrawaddy, joins the main stream at Myinmu below Sagaing on the right bank. It is largely used for irrigation purposes and waters thousands of acres of rice fields.

The greatest affluent of all is the **Chindwin**. Rising as the Tanai in the Hukong valley, north-west of Myitkyina, it flows past the Shan States of Singaling Hkamti and Hsawnghsup, through the two Chindwin districts, past Kindat, Mawlaik, Mingin and Mônywa, pursuing a winding course, with many a curve and many an eddy, till it enters the Irrawaddy above Pakôkku. It is navigable by light draught steamers and launches as far as Kindat throughout the year and up to Homalin (330 miles) in the rains; regular steamer services have long been established. But its course is impeded by shallows and whirlpools. The upper reaches flow through brilliantly picturesque, savage country clouded by myths and legends. It is said that above a certain point on the Chindwin though there are snakes they are not venomous. Less easily credible is the report of a village whereof the people can transform themselves into tigers. The main tributaries of the Chindwin are the Yu, Myittha and Kyaukmyet from the west and the Uyu from the east. Of these the most important is the Myittha into which flow the Maw from the south and the Manipur from the north.

Further south, on the right bank, the Irrawaddy receives the Yaw, in Pakôkku, the Salin, Môn and Man, in Minbu; on the left bank, the Pin which rises on Popa and joins the main river above Yenangyaung, and the Yin which runs for 120 miles from Yamèthin through Magwe. Besides the tributaries which have been specified, the Irrawaddy is fed by unnumbered mountain torrents of whose nomenclature the tediousness shall not be inflicted on the reader.

[1] Pronounced like the note of the cow not of the cat.

Rangoon River. The Rangoon river is important solely on account of the port after which it is called. Rising in the Prome district some 150 miles from its mouth, under the name of Myitmaka it flows through Prome and Tharrawaddy, taking further down the name of Hlaing, and passes Rangoon, twenty-one miles from the sea. Not far below Rangoon it is joined by the Pegu river which flows for 180 miles, past the historic town of Pegu; and by the Pazundaung river. The Panlang creek above Rangoon has already been mentioned. A little below the town, a serious obstacle to deep draught steamers, is the Hastings Shoal which seems to resist the efforts of dredgers.

Bassein River. The Bassein or Ngawun river has been mentioned as a branch of the Irrawaddy. Leaving the main stream above Henzada, it flows for 200 miles, past Nga-thaing-gyaung and Bassein to the sea at Diamond Island. It is navigable for sea-going steamers as far as Bassein. Its affluents are the Daga above, the Panmawadi below, Bassein.

Salween. Almost parallel with the Irrawaddy and exceeding it in length is the Salween. Rising in remote unvisited hills in China, it emerges in the Shan States which it traverses for many miles, receiving among other tributaries, the Nam-ting, Nam-kha, Nam-bin, on the left, the Nampaung, Namtung (250 miles), Nam-pawn (300 miles), on the right bank. Thence it enters and intersects Karenni and flows past the hill district of Papun or Salween which it separates from Siam. On the edge of the Thatôn district the Thaungyin, rising in the Dawna hills, joins it from the south-east. Crossing Thatôn and Amherst, after receiving the waters of its main tributaries the Yônzalin from the north and the Gyaing (formed by the union of the Hlaingbwe and Haungtharaw) and Ataran from the south-east, the Salween enters the Gulf of Martaban, 28 miles below Moulmein, after a course of about 650 miles in British territory. The Salween is a swift stream flowing for great part of its course between steep rocky banks which rise in places from 3000 to 5000 feet above the river level. A little below the junction with the Thaungyin, navigation is peremptorily checked by the impracticable rapids of Hatgyi. Though many plans have been suggested, it seems unlikely that means of utilizing the Salween for steamer traffic will be devised. It is, however, of great value as a timber floating stream, bringing to the depot at Kado above Moulmein teak from the forests of the Shan States, Karenni, Siam, Thatôn and Amherst. The beauty of its scenery has often been celebrated.

Mèkong. Although the Burmese kingdom extended across the Mèkong, all territory to the east of that river has long been abandoned. The Mèkong now forms part of the boundary of the Shan States dividing Kēngtūng from French Indo-China. After flowing for many miles parallel to the Salween, it turns eastward and discharges its waters into the China Sea.

Sittang. The Sittang or Paunglaung, a river of some importance, rises in Yamèthin and traverses the Tenasserim Division from north to south, passing the towns of Toungoo and Shwegyin and dividing Pegu from Thatôn, pursuing a course of 350 miles to the Gulf of Martaban. At uncertain times, a bore or tidal wave runs up from the sea, at a height of 9 feet and the rate of 12 miles an hour, with disconcerting effect. This bore is well described by Cæsar Frederick. It is still as vigorous as ever and has cut through the Sittang-Kyaikto canal which in consequence has been abandoned.

Minor rivers in Tenasserim are the Great Tenasserim, Lenya, and Pak-chan in Mergui; and the Tavoy river in the district of that name.

In Arakan the only important river is the Kaladan which rises in the Chin Hills as the Boinu. It follows a tortuous course through the Chin country and the Lushai Hills; thence more regularly southward through Northern Arakan to the sea at Akyab, having a total length of about 300 miles. In Akyab it is navigable by river steamers.

Fig. 18. Boinu River.

Lesser rivers in Arakan are the Lemru, Mayu and Naaf in Akyab; the An and Dalet in Kyaukpyu; the Mai,

Tanlwe, Taungup, Sandoway and Gwa in Sandoway; none of any great importance.

Besides rivers properly so called, multitudinous mountain torrents, dry for months, suddenly swelling into rushing streams and as rapidly subsiding, abound in all the hills and adjacent plains. No useful purpose would be served by an enumeration of these fleeting water courses, even if an exhaustive catalogue could be compiled.

CHAPTER IV

MOUNTAINS AND HILLS

PEOPLE who speak and write of Burma as a rule get their impressions from the most highly developed, and therefore most easily accessible, deltaic region and Irrawaddy valley. But the land of plains and swamps is but a fraction of Burma which is mainly a country of rugged hills and mountains. Though the topmost heights are far below the towering peaks of central Asia, there are many mountains of quite respectable eminence.

East of the Irrawaddy, starting from the north, the Eastern Kachin Hills run southward from Tibet occupying the eastern part of Putao, Myitkina and Bhamo and dividing those districts from China, a maze of hills and mountains some 30 to 35 miles in breadth, with peaks 3000, 7000 and 11,000 feet in height. South of these are the hills of the Ruby Mines, with the outstanding peaks of Taungme (7544 feet) and Shwe-u-daung (6231 feet). Bernardmyo, hard by, is on a height of nearly 6000 feet and Mogôk, the centre of the ruby-mining industry, is about 4000 feet above the sea. The hills dividing Burma proper from the Shan States rise to heights of 4700 feet in Mandalay, 5000 feet at Nat-teik in Kyauksè, and 6000 feet in Yamèthin. Rising from the plains of Myingyan are isolated groups of hills. Popa (5000 feet) in the south-west of the district, a double peak of volcanic origin, has already been mentioned as a conspicuous landmark. It is also famous as the haunt of *nats*[1] of great repute.

In Yamèthin rises the **Pegu Yoma**, running thence southward approximately through the middle of Lower Burma and forming the watershed between the Irrawaddy

[1] See p. 129.

and the Sittang. Its heights are inconsiderable, hardly exceeding 2000 feet. Gradually declining, it ends with the hill crowned by the Shwe Dagôn Pagoda at Rangoon.

Fig. 19. Shwe Dagôn Pagoda.

To the east, on the great Shan plateau, itself averaging in height from 3000 to 4000 feet, are countless hills and many mountain chains. Dividing North and South Hsenwi is the Loi-Hpa-Tan range, with the high peak of Loi-sak (6000 feet); in east Hsipaw, the Loi-Pan group, rising to nearly 7000 feet; in South Hsenwi, Loi-Leng (9000 feet). In Tawngpeng to the northward, a mass of hills, the loftiest range rises to 7500 feet. East of the Salween, the hilly tract of Kokang has heights of over 7000 feet; south of this is a tangled maze of hills. In the Southern Shan States, five separate ranges run approximately north and south with many conspicuous peaks, Sindaung and Myinmati (each 5000 feet) on the western border; Ashe-myin-anauk-myin in the Menetaung range; Loi Maw and Loi Mai (each 8000 feet).

East of the Pegu Yoma, in Toungoo the Paunglaung and Nattaung ranges rise above 5000 feet. The Paunglaung continues southward into Thatôn. On the Siamese border are the hills forming the Salween district, with heights from 3000 to 5000 feet. Thatôn and Amherst have the Dawna range and the Taung-nyo range which ends as the Martaban Hills; and in Thatôn the Kelatha Hills take off from the Paunglaung and attain heights of 3650 feet. Further south, the inland parts of Tavoy and Mergui consist of hill ranges extending eastward to the frontier of Siam, in which the highest peaks are Myinmoletkut (6800 feet) and Nwalabo (nearly 6000 feet).

West of the Irrawaddy, the Kinwun range runs from Hkamti-lōng, east of Assam, culminating in the peak of Shwe-daung-gyi (5750 feet) near Mogaung. South of Mogaung are the Kauk-kwe Hills and the Loi-yet range. Further south, Katha has many hills, the best defined ranges being the Minwun which takes off from Taungthônlôn far to the north, with the height of Maing-thôn (5450 feet) and the Gangaw, parallel to the Irrawaddy, rising to 4400 feet.

In the extreme north, on the edge of Tibet, are superb chains of mountains culminating in a mighty peak, as yet unnamed, 19,764 feet in height, at the limit of the Putao district. Other peaks in or on the borders of Putao attain heights of 11,000, 12,000 and 14,000 feet. The district itself, save for the plain of Hkamti-lōng, is a mass of hills and mountains. In the north-west, on the borders of Singaling

Fig. 20. The road to Kalaw.

Hkamti, lofty hills separate Burma from Assam. Here is Nwemauktaung or **Saramati** (12,557 feet), long regarded as the highest peak in Burma but now known to be dwarfed by the giant of Putao. From this mass of hills branches the Pôndaung range, running southward through Upper and Lower Chindwin and Pakôkku, with heights from 2000 to

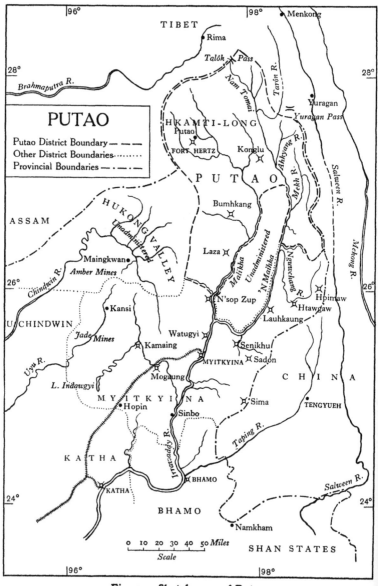

Fig. 21. Sketch map of Putao.

4000 feet. The hills forming the watershed between the Irrawaddy and the Chindwin start in the extreme north and run south-south-west, averaging not more than 1000 feet in height but rising to over 5000 feet in Taungthônlôn in Upper Chindwin. Other ranges of moderate altitudes traverse Lower Chindwin and Sagaing.

The Chin Hills, bordering on Assam and Manipur, have already been mentioned as nothing but a maze of mountains. The main ranges run north and south, the principal being the Letta or Tang, the Inbuklang, and the Kong Klang, varying from 5000 to 9000 feet in height. West of Pakôkku, the southern part of the Chin Hills has heights from 5000 to 7000 feet, with the great peak of **Mt Victoria** (10,400 feet). In the Arakan Hill Tracts, the heights dwindle to 3000 and 3500 feet, but the best defined range, Kyauk-pan-daung, rises to 4500 feet. Taking off from the Chin Hills, skirting Minbu, the **Arakan Yoma** separates Arakan from the plains of Irrawaddy and ends at Cape Negrais. Other ranges in Arakan are the Mayu, between the Naaf and Mayu rivers, and two ranges between the Kaladan and Mayu.

As pointed out in the chapter on Geology, the oro-graphical relief of Burma is still a rough expression of relatively young earth movements, although the rock folds, since their formation, have been superficially scored and mutilated by recent weather action, and the underground structure has thus been obscured, just as a description of the country must necessarily be obscured by the use of many unfamiliar names. The westward movement of the solid block of old rocks forming the Shan plateau, meeting the southerly creep towards India of the Tibetan plateau, has formed the sigmoidal curves of the Irrawaddy valley, the general north-south trend of the oil-fields, the Arakan and Chindwin ridges and even the western sea shore, all features of relief roughly parallel to one another in direction and at right angles to the great earth movements in which they originated.

CHAPTER V

ISLANDS

In the seas surrounding Burma are innumerable islands, for the most part of no great economic importance. Some will be mentioned in the short account of lighthouses.

At the mouth of the Kaladan, off the coast of Arakan, are the Baronga Islands where oil wells have been worked for many years with only moderate success. Further south, forming great part of Kyaukpyu, are the large inhabited islands of Ramree (800–900 square miles) and Cheduba (220 square miles) and many smaller islands. Off the coast of Sandoway is Foul Island. At the mouth of the Bassein river are Haing-gyi or Negrais and Diamond Island where countless turtles lay myriads of eggs.

For five months of the year, Diamond Island is swept by cyclones, blinded with prodigious rain; its little houses are tethered with thick steel ropes against the assaults of tremendous gales. But at the right season and in its own way Diamond Island is perfection. During seven dry months its climate is simply that of the Island Valley of Avilion. It is girded with splendid sands, and in certain places low rocks project from the edge of the sand into the sea....From the landing place a path leads up a low cliff and runs across the island through park-like lawns and woods. Barking deer sport in its charming glades....The grass is always green and the water brooks fail not[1].

The serpent of this Eden is the deadly sea-snake of the encircling waters.

Attached to the Hanthawaddy district for administrative purposes are the Cocos, two islands of no great size or importance, lying nearly due north of the Andamans[2].

[1] Marjorie Laurie.
[2] The Andamans and Nicobars are not part of Burma.

The sea bordering on Tavoy is studded with small islets, the most noticeable, the three groups of Moscos, uninhabited save by builders of edible birds' nests; the largest, Tavoy Island. All along the coast of Mergui are the multitudinous clusters of the famous **Mergui Archipelago** hardly rivalled for picturesque beauty. Of these islands, 804 in number, the largest and almost the only one inhabited by civilized people is King Island (170 square miles) whereon is a rubber plantation. To enumerate others would be merely to give a catalogue of names. Many of these islands are the home of a strange people known as Salôn or Mawken, by some called sea-gypsies[1]. Here are pearl fisheries, mentioned elsewhere.

[1] A full account of these people is given in *The Sea Gypsies of Malaya* by Walter Grainge White, F.R.G.S.

CHAPTER VI

LAKES

THE largest lake is **Indawgyi** in Myitkyina, covering an area of 80 square miles. Surrounded on three sides by

Fig. 22. Royal Lake, Rangoon.

wooded hills, its placid waters present a scene of unsurpassed loveliness. Seldom visited in former years, it was a favourite theme of legend and romance. Fair floating islands moved upon its bosom and the fabled unicorn roamed on its grassy borders. These roseate visions have vanished, but the perfect beauty of Indawgyi is not a dream or myth.

In the Shan State of Yawnghwe is the large and famous
Inle lake. Here are lake-dwellers, amphibious progeny
of captive Tavoyans, who practise the curious art of
paddling, by holding the paddles with their legs.

Other lakes of note are Indaw (60 square miles) in Katha;
Shwepyi and Taungthaman in Mandalay; Mahananda,
Halin, Kadu and Thamantha in Shwebo; Ye-myet in
Sagaing (10 miles by 3); the large artificial lake of Meiktila,
constructed under the orders and immediate supervision
of King Bodawpaya rather more than a hundred years ago;
Inma in Prome (10 miles by 4); Inye in Bassein (7 miles in
circuit). In Rangoon, the Royal Lakes in Dalhousie Park,
memorable for beauty and association, and the Victoria
Lake, a fine stretch of water, were both made by hands.
The Royal Lakes were made after the acquisition of Pegu
in 1852. The Victoria Lake, completed in 1884, had the
utilitarian object of providing the water-supply of Rangoon.
This does not render it less picturesque.

In most districts are to be found shallow meres, teeming
in due season with water-fowl.

CHAPTER VII

GEOLOGY

A STUDY of the present-day topography of a country would be incomplete without an enquiry into the steps by which that topography had been produced. The contemplation of the coast-line, mountain ranges, valleys, river-systems, fauna, flora and climate of any particular region awakes in us a keen curiosity as to the various changes in configuration and meteorological conditions which have made up the past history of that region. No contemporaneous brain has penned such a history, whose torn and disfigured pages are the rocks from which we try to reconstruct former conditions.

The first chapter of this most ancient book of Nature, in the case of Burma, consists of a belt of **gneiss**, a quartz-bearing rock which, under the influence of enormous pressure and high temperature, has assumed a banded streaky texture. This belt, commencing near Mandalay, extends northwards and north-westwards through the ruby mines of Mogôk into the country north of Bhamo and into the Chinese province of Yünnan; above Mogôk ranges formed of this gneiss culminate in the Taungme peak (7544 feet above sea-level). Folded up with the gneiss are beds of limestone in which the celebrated Burmese rubies and sapphires are found, but these pages of Burma's geological history are so blotted and blurred that we cannot decipher the conditions under which the limestones and some of the gneiss were produced. The former may represent sediments laid down on an ancient sea-bed, or they may be deposits formed after the consolidation of the surrounding rocks by percolating solutions of carbonate of lime. Some of the gneiss is solidified molten material, but

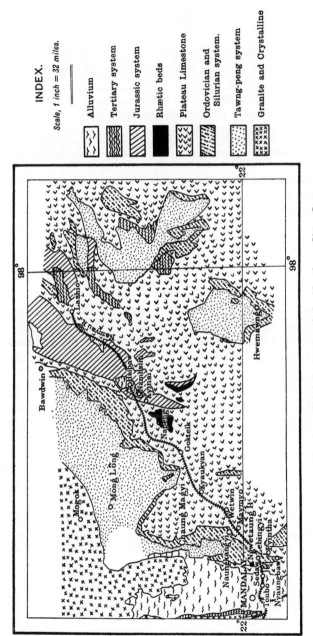

INDEX.

Scale, 1 inch = 32 miles.

Alluvium

Tertiary system

Jurassic system

Rhætic beds

Plateau Limestone

Ordovician and
Silurian system.

Tawng-peng system

Granite and Crystalline

Fig. 23. Geological map of the Northern Shan States.

W. B

4

whether it solidified underground as bosses and dykes or was ejected at the surface as volcanic matter it has not yet been possible to say. Much of this gneiss has been referred to the lowest horizons of the Archæan, the oldest geological system known, whilst other different types, together with the ruby-bearing crystalline limestones, show distinct resemblances to the Dharwar rocks of the Indian peninsula, which are metamorphosed sedimentary deposits of later Archæan age. A similar gneiss was observed in the Yaméthin district, and it is surmised that a more or less continuous belt of this rock extends from Yünnan to the vicinity of Moulmein. Intersecting in every direction the ancient Archæan gneisses are veins of granite which in a molten state has been forced into fissures.

The next oldest rocks have so far yielded no fossils, and must belong either to the Cambrian—*i.e.* the oldest known fossil-bearing system—or to an intermediate system between the Cambrian and the more ancient Archæan, or to both. They comprise what has been called the **Tawng-peng system** in the Shan States and the **Mergui beds** of Tenasserim. Whatever their precise age may be, their most characteristic feature is the complete absence of lime, the rocks consisting of schists, various altered forms of sandstone and clay, and an interesting series of lava flows and volcanic ashes ejected from neighbouring vents. The lavas in the Shan States strongly resemble similar lavas found in the Malani district of the Jodhpur State in Rajputana and are of much the same age. Amidst the volcanic ashes and lavas occur the important lead, silver, zinc and copper deposits of Bawdwin. In Tenasserim the Mergui beds, which probably form a more or less continuous belt with those of the Shan States, are also associated with rich mineral deposits, but in this case of wolfram and tin[1]. The Mergui beds are no greater in bulk than the granite which has been intruded into them. This granite has been

[1] See p. 74.

traced as far north as Yamèthin and is very probably continuous with a broad belt of the same rock in the Kyauksè district. A different kind of granite containing the mineral tourmaline has been injected into the schists of the Tawngpeng system in the Ruby Mines sub-division and is also found associated with the Mergui beds of Tenasserim.

The Tawngpeng rocks formed a continuous floor on which the fossiliferous sediments of the Palaeozoic ocean were deposited. There is some interesting evidence by which it seems probable that the Tawngpeng rocks in the Shan States area projected here and there above the surface of this ocean in the form of islands, for some of the sediments of the Palaeozoic ocean thin out in a remarkable way as they approach these islands, and frequently overlap older sediments below. An example of one of these islands is the mountain mass of Loi Leng.

The records which follow thrill one with their clearness and their absorbing interest. They are scored on rocks which contain a rich fauna generally similar to that found in the rocks of North Wales and on that account termed the **Ordovician system**. The largest exposure of these rocks is to be seen about 11 or 12 miles east of Mandalay. Their fauna includes specimens of the stalked, bud-like, extinct animals known as cystids, many species of brachiopods—bivalve shell-fish of which one shell covers the back and the other the belly—including more than one identical with European forms, and many remains of the curious, extinct, primitive crustaceans known as trilobites. The earlier sediments of this system are homogeneous over wide areas in the Shan States, and indicate an open sea of uniform but no great depth, with a coast-line somewhere to the west. The later deposits are crowded with shell fragments and the detached eyes of trilobites, and were evidently laid down in a sea teeming with life. Perhaps the most interesting point about the Burmese Ordovician, however, is the relationship of its fauna to that of other

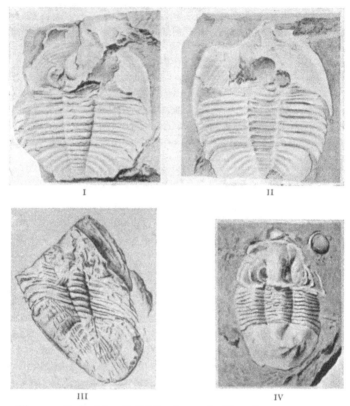

Fig. 24. Ordovician Trilobites from the Shan States; the third specimen has been distorted by pressure.

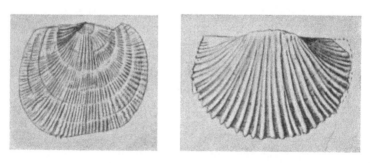

Fig. 25. Ordovician brachiopods from the Shan States.

Ordovician exposures. It is found that this fauna resembles much more closely the Ordovician fauna of North Europe, especially of the Baltic provinces, than it does that of the central Himalaya. The Ordovician of the Himalaya in Spiti and Kumaon contains no cystids and extremely few trilobites, and its fauna generally resembles that of the American beds of the same age. We are constrained, therefore, to make the interesting deduction that in Ordovician times the Arctic sea which covered what is now Northern Europe, extended into Burma as far south as latitude 21° N., and was separated from the sea which covered the central Himalaya. The former sea spread over central and north-eastern China, but of its southern limit we know nothing as yet.

Lying upon the Ordovician are shales, sandstones and limestones of no less interest and importance. These beds, from the character of their rich fauna, belong to a system known as the **Silurian**, after an area in South Wales in which they were first studied. As in the Ordovician, trilobites and brachiopods are common, but the occurrence of most interest is that of the peculiar rod-like colonies of animals known as graptolites; these were found for the first time in Asia by Mr T. D. La Touche in December, 1899. The discrepancy between the Burmese fauna and that of the central Himalaya and America, noted in the case of the preceding system, is still more strongly marked in the Silurian. About 87 per cent. of the Burmese forms are identical with or allied to European forms, while only 35 per cent. are so related to America; only seven forms are common to Burma and the central Himalaya, and these are all ubiquitous forms. The Himalayan forms are allied to American and European in practically equal proportions. The central Himalayan fauna includes no graptolites and is predominated by corals, most of which have marked American affinities, while the Burmese fauna is characterized by abundant graptolites, several of which are identical with those of Great Britain, and only one coral. We are justified in concluding, therefore, that the two Ordovician oceans remained separate from each other throughout Silurian times also. The southern extension of

Fig. 26. Fault Scarp at Pong Wo, Northern Shan States.

the Silurian ocean which covered the Shan States is not yet known.

The uppermost Silurian beds pass up into a great limestone system which has been termed the **Plateau Limestone** from the fact that it forms the great undulating plateau of the Shan States. Visitors to Maymyo will be familiar with the typical scenery belonging to this system, rolling uplands covered by a thick mantle of poor red clay soil on which the common bracken fern flourishes, shallow valleys or precipitous gorges, and steep cliff-scarps due to faulting. The limestone, when freshly broken, has, like so many limestones, a fœtid smell. It usually includes a proportion of carbonate of magnesia, and in fact varies from a pure lime carbonate to a true dolomite. The rock is characterized by a network of calcite veins, which have evidently filled an innumerable series of fissures, and give the rock such an unstable texture that one blow from a hammer will often shatter a small boulder into fragments, a quality much appreciated by those in quest of road-metal or railway ballast; as the limestone has not been excessively folded this peculiar fracture structure must be regarded as the direct result of pressure, exerted after the consolidation of the limestone and caused by the great earth movements which commenced just before the Tertiary period. Fossils are not frequent but from the small assemblage of forms so far collected, the great bulk of the Plateau Limestone belongs to the Devonian system, and its fauna, incomplete as it is, seems to have more in common with the Devonian of Europe than with that of America. The Plateau Limestone in all probability extends continuously to Moulmein and Tenasserim, and similar limestones have been described in Yünnan and other parts of China. Mr La Touche concluded that the Plateau Limestone was formed under conditions similar to those of modern coral reefs, and that some of the ranges, such as Loi Leng and the Loi Pan-Loi Twang range, may have been islands in the Devonian sea.

Here and there upon the plateau we find small patches of a limestone which differs in many ways from the great bulk of the beds below, and in some places contains abundant fossils. An examination of the latter shows that these patches are younger than the underlying massive lime-stone, and correspond to the middle and upper **Permo-Carboniferous** of the Salt Range in the Punjab and of the Ural Mountains. The most significant points are the identity of many of the species with central Himalayan fossils, and of a few with Malayan forms, and a closer resemblance of the fauna to that of America. The Permo-Carboniferous ocean of the Shan States seems to have been connected in one direction with that of Malaysia, and in another direction with that of the central Himalaya and America.

During the next phase the coral reefs of the Devonian and Permo-Carboniferous, at least in the Shan States, were raised by a gentle earth-movement, which caused the sea to retreat leaving a land surface subject to the denuding agencies of the atmosphere. This land phase in the Shan States lasted throughout all but the lower part of the **Permian** and all but the uppermost part of the **Triassic** periods. Towards the end of this phase we find evidence of sea along the west of Burma, occupying what are now the Arakan Yoma and the Naga Hills, and to the north in Yünnan where the presence of beds of salt and coal points to shallow water conditions. After the coral-reef land of the Shan States had been worn by rain, rivers and other natural agencies into ridges and hollows, a gentle de-pression of the whole caused an invasion of the sea, which filled up the hollows with fine sediments. Some of these hollows maintained a connection with the open sea while others seem to have been more or less completely cut off as salt lakes. The amenities of aquatic life, therefore, varied considerably, and we find in some localities badly developed, stunted forms typical of restricted conditions, and in more salubrious spots well-favoured massive forms. These fossils have been identified as belonging to the upper-most Trias (**Rhaetic stage**), and a similar fauna has been found to the north in Yünnan and to the south in the Malay States and Sumatra.

The Shan States remained part of a shallow sea extending into China throughout the next period, the **Jurassic**, but was raised to dry land for the last time at its close. The Jurassic sea probably extended westward, covering the area now occupied by the Arakan Yoma and Naga Hills, but seems to have had no connection with a contemporaneous sea spreading at that time over the central Himalaya and Cutch.

The period which follows the Jurassic is known as the **Cretaceous** and precedes the Tertiary. During the Cretaceous period a widespread system of earth-movements was initiated which lasted throughout the Tertiary and does not appear to have quite ceased at the present day. The configuration of Asia was greatly affected thereby and the present system of mountains and valleys in Burma is entirely due to one of these corrugating movements. India, before these movements took place, formed part of a vast continent known as Gondwanaland which included a large part of Africa. One portion of the coast-line of this continent coincided approximately with the present east coast of India, but extended north-eastwards along the southern margin of the Shillong plateau and Mikir Hills up to the north-east corner of Assam, where it probably curved round and joined the western margin of the Shan plateau, passing southwards in a sigmoidal curve close to Moulmein and the present coast of Tenasserim and Malaysia. The sea bordering this coast was in fact an enlarged precursor of the present Bay of Bengal. At the same time another sea covered Tibet and stretched as far eastwards as Sikkim. Whether these two seas were ever connected is doubtful. The only part of Burma which formed dry land at this time, therefore, comprised Tenasserim, Karenni, the southern and northern Shan States, and the Kachin country, connected through Yünnan with the Gondwana continent of India and Africa. The Chindwin valley, the whole of the Irrawaddy valley excepting the uppermost portion, and probably the whole of the Naga Hills and Arakan Yoma, as well as the Andaman and Nicobar Islands, were covered by the sea which formed the ancient Bay of Bengal.

Two of the earth-movements mentioned above have now to be considered, one from the north and one from the east, both advancing towards the centre of the Indian peninsula. By **the movement from the north** the northern margin of the Gondwana continent was folded again and again into the mighty mass of the Himalaya, the Tibetan sea retreating westwards until central Asia became dry land. In front and along the foot of this mountain mass was a deep trough, which at first formed a long gulf, but which subsequently became filled up with river sediments, and now coincides with the Ganges valley and portions of the valleys of the Indus tributaries. There is some evidence to show that behind the mountain mass was another less pronounced trough separating the mountain range from the Tibetan table-land, and that this was also occupied successively by a gulf and a river. **The movement from the east** produced an almost exactly similar effect upon Burma. The Shan plateau may be looked upon as corresponding to the lofty Tibetan table-land, the Arakan Yoma and Naga Hills take the place of the Himalaya, the Chindwin-Irrawaddy valley is the smaller trough behind the mountain mass, and the Arakan coast and the valley of the Meghna river which originally stretched into Upper Assam represent the large trough in front. Each of the two troughs, as in the case of the Himalayan troughs, was occupied successively by a gulf and a river, the rivers being the Chindwin-Irrawaddy (for the Chindwin was originally the head-waters of the main river) and the old Meghna. The point of interference between the two great movements just described was the north-eastern corner of Assam; here the mountain ranges of the two systems veer round till they confront one another in more or less parallel lines. One small difference between the two areas is that, whereas

Fig. 27. The Chindwin River.

the Himalaya is a simple curve convex towards the
direction of the compressional force, the Naga Hills and
Arakan Yoma with the Andamans and Nicobars form a
well-marked double S-shaped curve.

It is difficult to say precisely when the Naga Hills and
Arakan Yoma first began to appear from beneath the waters
of the old Bay of Bengal, but the Meghna and Chindwin-
Irrawaddy gulfs seem to have been separated off from each
other early in the Tertiary period; in these two gulfs were
deposited the oil-bearing sediments which to-day are being
tapped at various spots along the Arakan coast and at
different localities in the Irrawaddy and Chindwin valleys.
The movement from the east corrugated the floors of the
gulfs and caused their silting up. A river in each case
succeeded them and its sediments also were folded by the
continued movement. This east-to-west movement is the
key to all the present topography of Burma, and is the
reason for the north-to-south sigmoidal direction of its
mountain ranges and valleys. The Andaman and Nicobar
Islands are an extension of the Arakan Yoma and are
connected with it by a submarine shelf or ridge. The
Chindwin river is thought to have been continuous at the
end of the Tertiary period with the Tsanpo or Upper
Brahmaputra, which was subsequently captured by the
Assam Brahmaputra.

At the close of the "gulfs" period several **volcanoes**
made their appearance, chief among which was the
mysterious and legend-haunted hill of Mt Popa, which
rises in lofty solitude from the plains of Myingyan. Its
earliest lava flows were covered by river sediments, but
subsequent ejections of lavas and ashes have piled a cone
nearly 5000 feet above sea-level. Flows of a different type
occurred from other vents in the immediate neighbourhood,
and several craters, thought to have been produced by
gigantic explosions, are to be seen along the banks of the
Lower Chindwin.

Fig. 28. Mt Popa.

Fig. 29. "Mud volcano," Minbu.

The so-called "mud volcanoes" of Cheduba Island, Minbu and other places are of a totally different category and origin. They are not volcanoes in the correct sense of the term, but mere ejections of salt mud thrown out by the force of hydrocarbon gases and frequently accompanied by petroleum. They are, in fact, nothing more than the accompaniments of gas seepages, and are intimately associated with occurrences of oil. Through the stopping up of the vents, these mud eruptions are sometimes of explosive violence, and the friction of colliding stones with one another may set fire to the inflammable gas, producing a result still more closely resembling the fiery eruption of a true volcano. This has happened more than once in the case of the large "mud volcano" in the island of Cheduba off the Arakan coast.

The Tertiary plateau, as well as the higher-lying Shan plateau, is covered with a mantle of red clayey silt which passes here and there into a deposit of gravel. The still more recent clays and sands, which have produced and are still producing the deltas of the Irrawaddy and Sittang, constitute part of the last-written and still incomplete chapter in the history of Burma. What the end of this chapter will be and what other chapters will follow, who would dare to say?

CHAPTER VIII

MINERALS

THE very name of Burma is associated in our minds with rubies and other precious stones, and yet the combined value of the rubies, sapphires and spinels extracted from the mines in 1919 was not half that of the tin, not a quarter that of the tungsten or of the silver, less than a sixth of the value of the lead output, and less than one-sixteenth that of petroleum. Burma, although not a store-house to the fabulous extent ordinarily believed of precious stones, is undoubtedly the richest province in minerals of the Indian empire. It is now proposed to give an account of these minerals *seriatim*.

Burmese **Amber** varies in colour from a pale yellow to a dull brown, and resembles a variety found in Sicily in the possession of a peculiar fluorescence. It is heavier, harder and tougher than that obtained on the Baltic coast. It is conjectured that the resin from which it was formed exuded from trees which flourished during the "gulfs" period described in the preceding chapter (Miocene). It is found in the Hukong valley in the extreme north of Burma, where it is dug out of a blue clay at depths of from 20 to 40 feet below the surface. Mandalay absorbs most of the material, which is sold in the form of rosaries, ear-cylinders and other ornaments. When rubbed with a non-conducting cloth amber acquires a charge of electricity, our word for the latter being derived from *elektron*, the Greek word for amber. Its use for pipe, cigar and cigarette mouthpieces is due to a belief of the Turks, whose custom it is to pass the pipe from one to another, that no infection can be transmitted.

Antimony in the form of the sulphide, stibnite, is known in the hills behind Moulmein, and also in the Southern Shan

States, but none of these deposits is rich. Stibnite is used by oriental beauties for blackening the eye-brows.

Barytes, Heavy-spar or **Sulphate of Barium**, as it is variously called, has been discovered in considerable quantity at Bawdwin in the Northern Shan States, and is used as a flux in the smelting of the silver-lead ores. Barytes can also be used as a white pigment and as a body for certain kinds of paper and cloth.

Bismuth in small quantities is associated with the antimony found in the hills opposite Moulmein, and occurs in considerable amount at one spot in the mines of Bawdwin. Compounds of the metal are employed for medicinal purposes, and the metal itself is a constituent of certain alloys with an unusually low fusibility.

Burma is well off in **Building stones**. Limestone in almost unlimited quantity but of a somewhat brittle tendency occurs in the vicinity of Moulmein; another band of good quality is known in the Bassein district. A chocolate-coloured limestone has been quarried near Zibingyi between Mandalay and Maymyo. A beautiful white marble comes from the Sagyin Hills north of Mandalay, and is much used in the manufacture of carved images of Buddha and for ornamental purposes by the Burmans; a similar marble occurs in large quantities at Kyauksè, south of Mandalay, and in the Ruby Mines sub-division. The "Plateau" limestone of the Shan plateau is, most of it, only fit for road-metal. Laterite is a rusty-red rock and derives its name from its quality of being easily cut up into rectangular blocks (Latin, *later*, "a brick"); the great bulk of the Burma supply comes from the Irrawaddy valley. Yellow, purple and pink sandstones are quarried near Toungoo. The granitoid gneiss from the Thatôn quarries has been largely used on the Burma railways and for land reclamation in Rangoon. Lime is manufactured from limestone at Tônbo, not far from Mandalay, at Zibingyi and at Thayetmyo.

One mineral of which Burma has felt the lack most acutely is good **Coal**. Coal of a kind is plentiful and ubiquitous enough, but it is always a Tertiary lignite, with low fixed carbon and high ash and water percentages. The best known seams occur in the Northern Shan States, in

Fig. 30. Gold washing in the Chindwin River.

the foothills of the Arakan Yoma in the Minbu and Henzada districts, and on the Kale river in the Upper Chindwin district. In the Shan States the Lashio and Namma fields are the most important, the latter possessing very large reserves of a lignite of less inferior quality.

Rich **Copper** ore has been discovered in the silver-lead

mines at Bawdwin. Little is known as to the quantity available but this is probably large.

Gold is found in a large number of the Burma rivers and streams, but its extraction has not proved a lucrative industry owing to lack of concentration. At the beginning of the present century dredging operations were commenced in the Irrawaddy and two of its branches in the Myitkyina district, but although the total output reached 9041 ounces in 1909, the venture was recently abandoned. A mine which promised good results was worked for some time at Kyaukpazat in Katha, but in the end failed to prove remunerative.

Gypsum is a soft, white or transparent mineral from which plaster of Paris is made. In the form of scattered transparent flakes it is widely disseminated in the lower Tertiary rocks of the Irrawaddy basin, but is not made use of to any extent. Mixed with cement gypsum confers the property of slow setting.

Iron ores, mostly of lateritic origin, are found and worked on a small scale in many parts of the Province. At Wetwin, near Maymyo, the deposits are comparatively extensive and are being exploited and used for fluxing purposes in the smelting of the Bawdwin silver-lead mines. Similar deposits exist at Twin-ngè.

A mineral very closely resembling jade and known as **Jadeite** has, for a very long time, been extracted in the form of rounded boulders from a yellow or orange clay at Tawmaw and Hweka, and from river mines at Mamôn on the Uyu, all in the Myitkyina district. It is derived from dykes in serpentine which have been intruded therein under great pressure. The working is still by primitive native methods. The stone is exported in large blocks by way of Mogaung and Kindat where an *ad valorem* duty is levied, the right of levying being farmed out by Government. The farmer assesses the value of the stone; the owner may either pay duty on the assessment or require the farmer to buy the stone at his own valuation. In 1921, 3815 cwts. of jadeite were extracted. White, green and blood-red varieties are obtained, and most of the output is sold to Chinese who attach magic properties to the stone. The green variety is the best known[1].

The **Lead-silver** mine of Bawdwin in the Northern Shan States is one of the richest of its kind in the world. Numerous old Chinese workings are to be seen scattered

Fig. 31. Chinese furnaces for the smelting of silver and lead at Bawdwin.

round the neighbourhood, and, according to an old inscription, were being operated as long ago as 1412 A.D., during the Ming dynasty. The extensive lines of entrenchments still to be seen on the heights of the surrounding hills, testify to the tenacity with which these old mines were held against invading Kachins from the north. The ore for the most part consists of a silver-bearing sulphide

[1] "Green as the most translucent jade (which has a hue incomparably fairer and sweeter than an emerald can show)." E. Œ. Somerville and Martin Ross.

of lead or galena, containing also a considerable proportion of zinc. The objective of the Chinese smelters seems to have been the silver, for the lead slag was left in heaps to be utilized ultimately by the Company at present working the mine. Between $17\frac{1}{2}$ and 54 ounces of silver to the ton are obtainable from the ore. The ores owe their present home to the compressional movement mentioned in the previous chapter. This movement has produced a zone of fracture, displacement and general disturbance along a north-to-south line passing through Bawdwin. Into this zone of broken rock mineral-bearing solutions have percolated and left their valuable deposits, especially within some decomposed and very ancient volcanic ash beds. The output of refined lead from these mines in 1921 was 33,717 tons, of fine silver 3,555,021 ounces.

Similar old silver-lead mines worked by the Chinese are described as occurring at Bhamo. Ore of this nature is known in the Amherst and Mergui districts, in the Southern Shan States, at Mt Pima in the Yamèthin district, and in the Yônzalin valley near the Salween.

The most valuable mineral Burma possesses is **Petroleum**, which is found in the Lower Tertiary beds of the Irrawaddy basin on the one side and of the Arakan coast on the other. These beds are, in fact, the "gulf" deposits mentioned in the chapter on Geology, and the formation of petroleum within them, perhaps from some form of vegetation, seems to be connected with the conditions produced by the silting up of the gulf. The desiccation caused the precipitation of gypsum and other sea-water salts, and the saline conditions established are thought by some to have directed the changes taking place in the decomposing vegetation of that period, and to have induced the formation of petroleum instead of lignite or coal. Whatever the original material was, petroleum accumulated in the porous sands of the Miocene period, and was prevented from escaping at the surface by thick caps of impervious clay. Any part of the porous sands not filled with petroleum or with the gas arising therefrom, was filled with water, most of which contained salts such as sodium sulphate, sodium chloride, magnesium sulphate, etc.; the oil being lighter than water would tend to float on the surface of the latter within the sands, and would always take up a higher position than the water unless prevented.

As the folding movement proceeded, these porous beds

Fig. 32. The Yenangyat Anticline, showing the arch.

with their protecting caps of clay became warped and folded into arches and troughs, the oil finding its way into the crests of the arches and the water occupying the troughs. In some cases the arches were folded so severely as to be fractured, most of the imprisoned oil thereby escaping. In places like Yenangyaung in the Magwe district, on the other hand, the arch is a gentle and undisturbed one, and vast quantities of petroleum have collected in the many porous sandstones beneath it. On this oil is exerted hydrostatic pressure by the water in the adjacent troughs, so that when the overlying clay-caps are pierced by the drill, the oil is forced up to the surface and frequently 100 or 150 feet into the air. At Singu and Yenangyat, on the Irrawaddy, some distance above Yenangyaung, the arch is not symmetrical as it is in the latter locality, but is much steeper on the eastern side than it is on the western. Two small fields, one in the Upper Chindwin and another at

Fig. 33. Native Oil Well in process of construction.

Minbu on the Irrawaddy, are yielding oil in small quantities. On the Arakan coast the production is more or less negligible. From Burmese crude oil we get petrol, illuminating oil, lubricating oil and wax for candles.

The most famous oil wells are at Yenangyaung, in Magwe. They have attracted the notice of all travellers who passed that way. Symes, who saw them in 1795, writes: "The celebrated wells of petroleum which supply the whole (Burmese) Empire and many parts of India....The mouth

Fig. 34. The Yenangyaung Oilfield.

of the creek was covered with large boats, waiting to receive a lading of oil.'' Long before that date, oil winning was a flourishing industry. In Burmese times, the wells were worked by crude native methods. They were owned by the workers known as *twinsas*[1], who were bound to sell the product at a stated price to the king's agent. In the year 1888, scientific methods were introduced by a Company which acquired wells by purchase, obtained concessions from Government, and sank many wells of their own. Since then the industry has very largely developed. Extraction is strictly controlled by Government, and elaborate regulations to ensure safety are enforced. A pipe line conveys the crude oil to Syriam, below Rangoon. In 1921, the output of petroleum from the whole province, principally from Yenangyaung, was 296·09 million gallons.

Gems. The greater part of the world's supply of **Rubies** comes from the Mogôk mines in Upper Burma. A few rubies, sapphires and spinels have been found at Sagyin near Mandalay, and at Nanyazeik in the Myitkyina district. At Mogôk rubies, many of the coveted pigeon-blood colour, accompanied by large quantities of bright red **spinel**, a few **sapphires** and occasionally beautiful blue crystals of **apatite**, are quarried from a gem-bearing gravel occurring at some depth below the alluvial valley floor. The gems are derived from lenticels of crystalline limestone closely associated with basic igneous rocks bands of which are folded up with the ordinary gneiss. Some think the limestone was derived from certain ingredients of the gneiss and was deposited from percolating solutions some time after the deposition or solidification of the gneisses. Others think that they were ordinary sedimentary limestones laid down upon and subsequently folded up with the gneiss. A few gems have been obtained from the limestone itself by driving cuttings into the hill sides or by excavations in fissures or hollows.

The ruby mines at and near Mogôk, some sixty miles

---

[1] Literally, eater (*i.e.* possessor) of a well.

north of Mandalay, have been worked by native methods from time immemorial. Cæsar Frederick (1569 A.D.) notes that the king "also is Lord of the Mines of Rubies, sapphires and spinels[1]." The rights of native miners have been preserved. But since 1886, the main work of extraction has been done by a Company with all the aids of science. The present plan is to wash and sift ruby earth (*byôn*) till all

Fig. 35. Burmese washing for rubies.

foreign matter is eliminated and only rubies and spinels remain.

Salt is manufactured from sea-water and also from the numerous salt springs found in many parts of the country especially in lower Tertiary beds. The Great War gave an impetus to salt extraction, an industry which was discouraged till recently. In 1919, about 70,000 tons were extracted, but in 1921 the output had fallen to 43,000 tons. It is doubtful whether, in normal times, the local produce can compete with foreign salt.

[1] Hakluyt, II. 365.

The efflorescence known in India as "reh," which frequently covers the exposed surface of the Tertiary beds, is often found to contain a certain proportion of **Carbonate of soda**. This impure carbonate, contaminated with sand and mud, is known as "soap-sand" and is used for washing purposes by the Burmans.

Steatite or **Soapstone** is found in several places in the Arakan Yoma associated with serpentine; the best known mines are in the Minbu district.

The Burma **Tin** belt of Tenasserim and that of the Federated Malay States are continuous, and together constitute one of the world's greatest tin resources. The ore is the oxide, cassiterite, and is found in the neighbourhood of masses of intrusive granite. The greater part of the ore won comes from alluvial deposits of gravelly clay derived chiefly from the decomposition of the granite.

A fine dark emerald-green **Tourmaline** is mined to a small extent at Namôn in Karenni, and pink, brown or black types are obtained at Maingnin in Mongmit. The pink variety known as **Rubellite** is also obtained from the ruby mines.

Tungsten in the form of the oxide, **Wolfram**, has been mined in both Tavoy and Mergui during the past ten years or so, and is found also in Southern Shan States, Karenni, and Thatôn. Like tin it is closely connected with granite and is found in the many quartz veins which traverse this granite and the ancient sediments into which the latter has been intruded. The chief use to which tungsten is put is that of hardening steel. It differs from other hardening agents such as chromium, vanadium, etc., in that scarcely any diminution of hardness results from a rise in temperature. For this reason it is an invaluable constituent of the steel required for high-speed tools, which preserve their cutting capacity in spite of the high temperature caused by friction. The demand occasioned by the war greatly stimulated wolfram mining. In 1918–19, the out-turn amounted to 4443 tons.

CHAPTER IX

FORESTS AND FLORA

THE forests of Burma may be conveniently classified as
(i) Evergreen, comprising (1) littoral, (2) swamp, (3) tropical,
(4) hill or temperate; and (ii) Deciduous, comprising (1) open,
(2) mixed, (3) dry. The littoral forests are confined to Lower
Burma, as also are, practically, the true swamp forests, while
the dry deciduous forests mostly occur in the Upper province.
The other classes are common to the whole of Burma. The mixed
deciduous forests yield most of the out-turn of teak. Large
areas covered entirely by teak are however not known and it
is rare even to find forests where teak is numerically the chief
species. As a rule it is scattered through forests composed of
the trees common to the locality. The *in* forests, so well known
on laterite formation, belong to the open deciduous sub-class,
while evergreen hill or temperate forests clothe a large proportion of the uplands of the Shan States. A considerable forest
area in Burma is covered with a luxuriant growth of bamboo[1].

The forests are among the most valuable sources of the
wealth of the Province. They are administered by Government through the agency of a skilled and highly trained
staff of Forest officers. The object of the administration is
the preservation of valuable trees, extraction on scientific
lines with due provision for reproduction so that the supply
of useful timber may not be exhausted, and the realization
of State dues. An elaborate Act and still more complex
Rules embody the principles of forest administration and
prescribe its methods.

Briefly, the theory is that all forest land and forest
produce belong to the State. But it is only over certain
land and in the case of certain produce that State rights
are fully enforced. There are two distinctions which must
be understood in order that the situation in respect of

[1] *Imperial Gazetteer of India—Burma,* I. 70.

forests may be realized. The first distinction is between ordinary public forest land and reserved forests. The second is between reserved and unreserved trees. It will be convenient briefly to deal first with the latter distinction. Certain trees of species which have an economic value are classed as reserved. These may not be cut on public forest land except under license. Teak, most valuable of all trees, is placed on a lonely eminence, its extraction being safe-guarded by stringent rules. Wherever it is found, growing teak is the property of the State, and may not be cut down without permission. But, except in the case of teak and of trees in reserved forests, much liberty is allowed to the people to use forest produce, even of reserved kinds, for domestic purposes. For trade, reserved trees can be utilized only under permit and on payment of forest dues.

Public forest land, which is estimated to cover 146,165 square miles, included at the end of 1919–20, 30,000 square miles of reserved forests. These reserved forests are tracts set aside normally for the production of timber or fuel, or in exceptional cases for protective reasons such as the maintenance of the water-supply. The settlement of a reserved forest is effected with extreme care. The intention to constitute a reserve is publicly notified. In due course, a civil officer, called the Forest Settlement officer, specially appointed for the purpose, aided by a Forest officer as adviser, makes a local investigation; hearing and adjudi-cating on all objections and claims to rights and privileges preferred by people living in or near the proposed reserve. His orders are subject to appeal to a higher civil officer. On the Forest Settlement officer's report, Government finally determines whether or not the proposed reserve is to be constituted. If the decision is in the affirmative, a final notification is issued, declaring the reserve constituted, defining its boundaries, and specifying any rights and privileges assigned to the neighbouring villagers. These rights and privileges consist for the most part of rights of way, rights to extract definite quantities of forest produce, rights of grazing fixed numbers of cattle. Subject to the rights and privileges specified in the notification, a reserved forest is the exclusive property of the State and is strictly protected from injury and trespass. The extraction of timber, principally teak, from reserves is regulated by elaborate working plans which provide for the exploitation of the forests by compartments and for due reproduction, so as to ensure a permanent supply. The extraction of timber is effected partly by contractors working directly under Forest officers, partly by large firms who hold leases of forests and pay royalty on the timber brought out. Among the most important and valuable teak forests are those on the slopes of the Dawna Hills and in the Thaungyin valley in Tenasserim; on the sides of the Pegu Yoma; on the hills east of the Sittang river; in Upper Chindwin, where thirty-three separate forests are recognized; in the Yaw drainage; in Bhamo, Katha, and Mandalay; in the Shan States and Karenni. The northern limit of teak is about 24° 30′ N. lat.; the southern limit between 15° and 16° N.

Teak is so intimately associated with Burma and so valuable a product that some space may be devoted to a description of the method of its extraction. Before teak can be extracted, the tree must be quite dead and dry. Almost always it has to be floated down streams; and green teak does not float. Therefore, two or three years before a forest is to be worked, a Forest officer goes through it, accompanied by a gang of coolies, and selects the trees which he considers fit for felling, taking care to leave a fair proportion of good seed-bearing trees for the purpose of regeneration. Each tree selected is ringed or, as it is technically called, girdled. The bark of the tree and the sap-wood are cut out in a circle so as to expose the heart-wood all round, the flow of sap being thus prevented. The trees are then left usually for three years till dry. Each of

these trees is carefully marked with a hammer, showing the
date of girdling, and a strict record of them is kept by the
Forest officer. The actual extraction is closely supervised
by that officer to whom accounts of extraction have to be
rendered. He also inspects from time to time and particularly, in the case of a leased forest, when the lessee
notifies that extraction is finished. It is part of his duty

Fig. 36. Forest-working elephants.

to satisfy himself that all girdled trees, if marketable, have
been extracted and that waste has not been committed in
logging them. It might seem to be quite easy to cut up a
tree into logs so as to ensure the greatest profit and the
least waste. But, as a matter of fact, logging is a difficult
operation and demands constant supervision by the European staff.

A forest is marked out into compartments. When work
is started one or two elephant camps are established in

each compartment. Each camp has an average of eight elephants, with a headman in charge. After being felled, the trees are cut into logs on the spot, a whole tree being too heavy for dragging. The logs are drawn by elephants to the nearest creek along rough roads generally made by elephants dragging the first logs. On arrival at the bank of the creek, the logs are measured and classified by the European staff and the result is reported to the lessee. The creeks which intersect the forest are very low in the cold and hot weather but are filled in the rains by big rises. After being measured and classified, the logs are launched as soon as possible so as to be ready for the next rise. Care must be taken not to crowd the logs, or they will jam at once, especially when, as is generally the case, the creek is narrow and tortuous. Always after a rise, two or three elephants are sent down the creek to put straight the logs and break up any jams. Unless the creek is exceptionally big, it takes a good many rises to float the logs into the main stream[1]. Later on, when they have reached the great river, the Irrawaddy, Salween, Chindwin, or Sittang, the logs are formed into rafts and floated down to Rangoon or Moulmein.

The Forest Department is administered on quasi-commercial lines and yields a substantial surplus. In the financial year 1920–21, the receipts were approximately £2,200,000, the expenditure £890,000, leaving a profit of £1,310,000.

Besides teak, many other trees of various economic importance abound. *Pyingado* (*Xylia dolabriformis*), harder than and nearly as durable as teak and, on account of its specific gravity, more difficult to extract, is used for railway sleepers and house-building. Other house-building woods are *pyinma* (*Lagerstroemia Flos Reginae*); *kanyin-byu* (*Dipterocarpus alatus*); *thitya* (*Shorea obtusa*); *in* (*Dipterocarpus tuberculatus*); *ingyin* (*Pentacme suavis*); *tauk-kyan* (*Terminalia tomentosa*); and *hnaw* (*Adina cordifolia*). *In* also

---

[1] Contributed by a worker in the forests.

yields resin. Another use of *pyinma* and *kanyin-byu* is for
boat-building, for which *kôkku* (*Albizia lebbeck*), *thingan*
(*Hopea odorata*), and *yamane* (*Gmelina arborea*) are also in
request. *Padauk* (*Pterocarpus macrocarpus*) is widely distributed. Economically its principal use is for the making
of cart-wheels; it is also much prized for gun-carriages and
for ordnance work generally. The roadside *padauk* (*Pterocarpus indicus*) is an introduced Malayan species not found
wild in the forests, a lovely tree, whose blossoms, when it
flowers three times just before the rains, fall in cataracts
of gold. Cutch or *sha* (*Acacia Catechu*) is common throughout the dry and comparatively dry districts and supports
a thriving industry. The wood is cut into chips, boiled, and
produces valuable tanning material. *Than* (*Terminalia
Oliveri*) and *dahat* (*Tectona Hamiltoniana*) are burnt for
charcoal. Extract of *than* has been used illegitimately for
adulteration of cutch. Pines (*Pinus Khasya*), best of resin-
producing trees, abound in the higher hills, notably in the
Chin country, the Shan States, the Ruby Mines, and
Salween; *Pinus Merkusii* is also found, mainly in the Shan
States and Salween. *Lac*, the excretion of the lac insect,
and *Chinese varnish* are produced in the Shan States. Oil
for torches is extracted from *Kanyin* (*Dipterocarpus alatus*
and *D. loevis*), black varnish from *thitsi* (*Melanorrhoea
usitata*). Of *thitkado* (*Cedrela Toona*) are fashioned sheaths
of native swords and daggers.

At the head waters of the Ngawchang, a tributary of the
'Nmaikha, is found a stately juniper from which the
Chinese make planks for coffins. It is described as a
magnificent tree, growing upwards of 150 feet in height
and over 20 feet in girth at the base[1]. The wood is white,
very fragrant, and smooth-grained[2]. The seat of the coffin
plank industry is at Kangpawng in Putao[3].

[1] *In Farthest Burma.* Captain Kingdon Ward, 113.
[2] *Handbook of Forest produce of Burma.* A. Rodger.
[3] W. A. Hertz, C.S.I.

A very beautiful tree is the Amherstia, thus pictured at the time of its discovery. "The only plant...which struck us as remarkable was a tree twenty-four feet high, abounding in long and pendulous pannicles of rich geranium-coloured blossoms, and long elegant lance-shaped leaves; it is of the class and order *Diadelphia Decandria* and too beautiful an object to be passed unobserved[1]." Declared

Fig. 37. Palms and Plantains.

to be a new genus, it was named "*Amherstia nobilis*, in compliment to the Countess of Amherst[1]."

Palms of all kinds flourish in luxuriant abundance and are characteristic features of the scenery everywhere in the plain country. Of these may be mentioned *dani* (*Nipa fruticans*) and *danôn* (*Calamus arborescens*), whose broad leaves are used for thatching; *tari* or *palmyra* (*Borassus*

[1] Crawfurd, 362.

flabellifer), from the fruit of which is extracted a liquor, pleasant and refreshing when newly drawn, highly intoxicant when fermented; coco-nut; and the small *thinbaung (Phoenix paludosa)* used for house-building. **Bamboos** for which the Burman has a thousand uses, abound in every district, the most notable species being *myinwa* (*Dendrocalamus Strictus*), *thaikwa* (*Bambusa Tulda*), *Kyathaung* (*Bambusa polymorpha*), *tinwa* (*Cephalostachyum pergracile*). Among innumerable varieties of grasses, canes, and reeds may be mentioned the fine *thin* reed (*Phrynium dichotomum*) of which are woven the beautiful mats of Danubyu; and *thetke* grass (*Imperata arundinacea*), commonly used for thatching. Valuable fibre is yielded by *Shaw* (*Sterculia* spp.).

Trees of minor importance are *kabaung* (*Strychnos nuxvomica*); *thitka* (*Pentace burmannica*); *tanaung* (*Acacia leucophloea*); and *kaunghmu* (*Parashorea stellata*). The india-rubber fig (*Ficus elastica*) is found in Myitkyina and beyond the administrative border.

Of little present economic value are the vast mangrove, swamp, and savannah jungles which thickly fringe the coast and tidal streams, abounding in dense bushes, creepers, elephant grasses, and reeds. The mangrove jungle of Hanthawaddy, which may be regarded as typical of the Delta

is characterized specially by *Bruguiera* and *Rhizophora*. Behind these forests and along the borders of tidal channels are the tidal forests, the most characteristic trees of which are *Sonneratia apetala* and *Avicennia tomentosa*. These forests have a thick scrubby growth, similar to that of the mangrove forests. *Nipa fruticans* and *Pandanus foetidus* form dense bushes, and *Phoenix paludosa* is very common. Creepers and climbers abound, including *Acanthus volubilis*, *Flagellaria indica*, etc.[1]

The mangrove forests may have a prospective value in supplying tan bark.

---

[1] *Imperial Gazetteer of India—Burma*, I. 242.

Miscellaneous wild growths are cardamums, cinnamon, castor-oil, gamboge, camphor, the paper mulberry (*Brousso-netia papyrifera*) from the bark of which Shan paper and Burmese *parabaik* are made, *thanat* in which is wrapped the native-made cheroot. *Letpan* (*Bombax malabaricum*), the silk cotton tree, is valued for its down. Characteristic of the dry zone of Upper Burma is the cactus, an intro-

Fig. 38. Tamarind trees.

duced plant which has become naturalized, often used as an impenetrable village fence.

Among wild growing fruit trees may be mentioned the mango, of no great value in its uncultivated state, jack (*Autocarpus integrifolia*), *Zi*, the wild plum (*Zizyphus Ju-juba*), *Zibyu* (*Phyllanthus Emblica*), Chinese date, tamarind, an introduced tree now widely spread.

In the hills **orchids** of countless varieties luxuriate in splendid profusion. The Chin Hills are clothed with rich masses of rhododendron, found also less abundantly elsewhere. On many mountain sides and upland plateaux are wild growths of temperate climes, oaks, yews, chestnuts, walnuts, crab-apples, pears, cherries, oranges, lemons, citrons, mulberries, figs, peaches, strawberries, roses, ivy, mistletoe and holly.

Lichens, mosses, and ferns abound. Of flowering plants, over 700 species are enumerated by General Collett, principally in the Shan States; among them *Ranunculus*, *Clematis*, *Viola*, *Swertia*, bushy *Lespedeza*, large flowering *Asters*, and showy *Ipomoea*. Of special note are *Schinia Wallichii*, with white camellia-like flowers; the wonderful *Rosa gigantea*, "particularly conspicuous, climbing over tall forest trees, from the top of which the long pendent branches, covered with very large white flowers, hang down in rich profusion"; *Lonicera Hildebrandiana*, "a conspicuous shrub with large, dark, glossy leaves and fine crimson flowers, seven inches long, and by far the largest of any known species of honeysuckle"; a tall *Lespedeza Pranii*, bearing "large dense panicles of fine blue flowers"; *Codonopsis convolvulacea*, with "beautiful dark blue convolvulus-like flowers"; *Ipomoea nana*, with flowers "large of a beautiful deep purple"; *Colquhounia elegans*, most beautiful of Labiatae with dark red and pale salmon-coloured flowers[1].

Anemone, mimosa, geranium, delphinium, magnolia, gardenia, campanula, primula, jasmine, gentians, lilies, also adorn this Paradise.

[1] General Collett. *Journal of the Linnaean Society*, XXVIII.

CHAPTER X

FAUNA.

Mammalia. Ungulata. THE fauna of Burma is singularly rich and varied. In nearly every district wander herds of elephants, from thirty to fifty, sometimes as many as a hundred, together, very destructive to crops, eating much and trampling down more. Except in the Shan States, they are strictly preserved and, save in defence of human beings or in protection of property, may not be shot without a license. The capture of wild elephants with the aid of tame elephants as decoys[1] was practised by Burmans probably from very ancient times, and certainly up to the extinction of the Burmese monarchy in 1885. The vivid account of kheddah[2] operations at Pegu in 1569 A.D. by the Venetian traveller, Cæsar Frederick[3], is an accurate description of similar operations at Amarapura in the time of the last king, more than three hundred years later. For some short time after the annexation of Upper Burma, the elephant-catching establishment was maintained. Later the somewhat primitive native method was abandoned and the capture of elephants on a large scale was undertaken by skilled and trained officers. Some years ago the Government Kheddah Department was abolished and, at present, the supply of elephants is left to private enterprise. The Burmese elephant is a useful beast, docile, and believed, perhaps erroneously, to be sagacious. He is not commonly used for riding and not at all on ceremonial occasions. As a baggage animal and for dragging timber

---

[1]   ...as Indians with a female
         Tame elephant inveigle the Male. HUDIBRAS.

[2] Kheddah—the stockaded enclosure into which the wild elephant is decoyed.

[3] Hakluyt, II. 362.

in the forest[1] he is exceedingly useful. When work is finished, dragging elephants are hobbled, their forelegs being tied together, and are then let loose in the forest to fend for themselves. Each has a wooden clapper round his neck to guide the riders when searching for them. Elephants thus hobbled often go quite a long way in a single night and are not at all impeded in their foraging. Though mechanical appliances have almost displaced them for this work, elephants are still used for piling teak logs in the timber yards of Rangoon and Moulmein and seem to display remarkable acuteness and intelligence. From time immemorial, the kings of Burma set much store on the possession of white elephants, regarding them as among the most honourable insignia of their royal state. Wars were waged for the possession of these precious beasts[2]. So far as Burma is concerned, the cult of the white elephant is dead.

Rhinoceros are found in several districts in Lower Burma but are not very common. The one-horned Javan (*R. sondaicus*) is rare; the two-horned Sumatran (*R. sumatrensis*) is more frequently encountered. The gaur, by some called the Indian bison (*Bos gaurus*), a handsome beast, standing as high as nineteen hands, is the largest of the wild oxen. Gaur are generally seen in herds. Forest lovers, they prefer hilly country. The banting or saing (*B. sondaicus*), the characteristic wild ox of Malay countries, is not uncommon in many parts of Burma. He is a very handsome beast, finer than the Javan variety, and may even be a distinct species. In habits he resembles the gaur but chooses lighter and more open forest and the outlying spurs of hills. Gaur have been found at heights above 5000 feet, saing not over 4000 feet. Of gaur and saing solitary bulls carrying fine heads are most eagerly sought by sportsmen. Both are often dangerous when wounded. The much discussed mithan (*B. frontalis*) is domesticated

---

[1] See p. 79.   [2] See p. 101.

in the Chin Hills and is well known in Putao and elsewhere
in the Province. Wild buffaloes, once fairly plentiful, are
now nearly extinct. The curious serow (*Nemorhoedus sumatrensis*), in appearance half donkey, half goat[1], is not very

Fig. 39. Bison.

common. The Burmans call him *taw-seik*, jungle goat, *taw-
myin*, jungle horse, or very inaptly *ka-ba-kya*, precipice
tiger[2]. Serow are goat-antelopes. They generally inhabit
heavy cover near rocky and dangerous ground and often

[1] Colonel G. H. Evans, C.I.E., C.B.E., V.D.
[2] But probably *kya* does not here mean tiger but has some connection
with *kya*, to fall.

lie out on cliffs under the shelter of rocks. They are very wary and hard to approach. The Burmese serow differs from the Himalayan tahr, also a serow, in having reddish, instead of white, stockings. The goral (*Urotragus evansi*), a small but true goat, has been identified in Upper Burma in comparatively recent years, but is not very common. Goral hang about precipitous ground and utter a peculiar whistle when alarmed.

Fig. 40. Mithan.

Most strange of all is the rare takin (*Budorcas taxicolor*), only lately encountered in Burma, though his horns were found in a Kachin village thirty years ago. He has been variously described as half goat, half buffalo; as looking like a small buffalo with curly or spiral horns; as a clumsily built ruminant, standing about as high as a small mule; as essentially a serow with affinities to the bovines through the musk-ox and other relationships to the sheep, goat, and antelope[1]. The first Englishman to shoot a takin was Mr C. H. Mears, travelling in Tibet with the late Mr J. W. Brooke. Mr Fergusson's description is interesting:

This little known animal stands as high as a small bullock, but is much more heavily built. Its legs are especially short and thick, and its feet are shaped like those of a goat, only much larger. I have seen some tracks as much as six inches in diameter. They have Roman noses, black curved horns, and short cut-off ears; the hair of the cow is creamy white, but most of the bulls have a reddish-grey coat, a short tail like a goat, and to some extent resemble the musk ox[2].

One is almost disposed to identify him with the tarand, "an animal as big as a bullock, having a head like a stag, or a little bigger, two stately horns with large branches, cloven feet, hair long like that of a furred Muscovite, I mean a bear, and a skin almost as hard as steel armour."

Takin are found at high altitudes in the lofty mountain ranges bordering on the north and east of the Putao district and not elsewhere in Burma.

Deer of four well-known species are abundant. These are *Thamin* (brow antlered deer, *Cervus eldi*), the handsome typical stag of Burma[3]; *Sat* (sambar, *C. unicolor*); *Dayè* (hog-deer, *C. porcinus*); and *Gyi* (barking deer, *Cervulus muntjac*). There are also small mouse deer, or chevrotain, of two kinds.

The tapir is rare, found only in Mergui, Tavoy, and Amherst. Wild pig are fairly common in most forest tracts; and do much damage to maize, millet, and other crops. Some of the old boars have tushes $9\frac{1}{2}$ inches long. The country is not suitable for pigsticking, which has never been adopted as a form of sport in the Province. Burmans have an ingenious method of getting rid of pigs damaging cultivation. At various parts of a field liable to incursion,

---

[1] *Game Animals of India.* Lyddeker, 157–158. *In Farthest Burma.* Kingdon Ward, 92.

[2] *Adventure, Sport, and Travel on Tibetan Steppes.* Fergusson, 140.

[3] Colonel G. H. Evans.

they place bamboo clappers, all attached to one long rope or cane of which the watchman in his observation post holds the end. Where pigs are known to enter no clapper is laid, but bamboo spikes of various lengths are planted with points directed inwards. When the pigs are in the field, the clappers are set in motion; the pigs rush to the place where there is no clapper-noise and get wounded by the bamboos. Next morning they can be tracked by dogs[1].

The so-called Burman pony is well known; a very useful,

Fig. 41. Bullocks with cart.

hardy animal, standing not more than $13\frac{1}{2}$ hands but capable of much work. He comes from the Shan States.

Burmese oxen, of the zebu or humped kind, are robust and sturdy beasts not differing in species (though probably a separate breed) from those in other parts of India, but conspicuous by their excellent condition. They are treated with great consideration, if not always with adequate knowledge. As Burmans usually do not drink milk, the calves get it all, much to their advantage. The normal

[1] Colonel G. H. Evans.

colour of Burmese cattle is red with white patches on the buttocks.

Carnivora. Tigers are to be found in all parts of the country. Though numerous they are not nearly so much in evidence as in many parts of India. This is perhaps due to the abundance of game in the large forests. In general Burmese tigers are more game than cattle killers. They have been reported to attack full grown elephants, but rarely. Man-eaters are by no means unknown. Within the last fifty years, on two separate occasions, tigers were shot in Rangoon, one in a crowded street[1], one on the side of the great pagoda. They had obviously strayed from their usual haunts and lost their way. Leopards or panthers are common in many parts of the province. They are much more inclined than tigers to hang about villages and human dwellings and kill dogs, calves, goats, even ponies and small oxen. Quite lately a leopard invaded Magwe, a small town in Upper Burma, and wounded several people. This visitation was a protest against the killing of cows, the worst mauled victim being the butcher. Burmans who, theoretically, do not kill any animal, and Hindus who reverence the cow, were ostentatiously spared. Black panthers have been shot but are very rare. About a dozen kinds of wild cats are described, of which the savage jungle cat and several civets including one which the Burmans call *kyaung-myin* or horse-cat (*Viverra zibetha*) and the clouded cat sometimes called the clouded panther, may be mentioned. Mongooses are not common. Jackals, though rare in most places, are plentiful enough in Akyab and have been found elsewhere. Wild dogs are numerous and widely distributed. They are found wherever there is game in a forest, generally near salt licks. They live in rather small packs and are excellent hunters, scaring away game to the annoyance of sportsmen. Whether there are any wolves in Burma is still a matter of controversy. Himalayan and

---

[1] This tiger was shot by Mr Arthur H. M. Middleton.

Malayan bears are met in many parts and in considerable numbers. Martens and hog-badgers are also to be found.

Rodentia. Squirrels of many kinds, flying and others, are abundant. So are rats and mice of half a dozen species. Porcupines are seen and in many places hares are plentiful.

Primates. Monkeys of about a dozen varieties include the white-handed and white-browed gibbon (the well-known hoolook), the crab-eating species, and three or four sorts of leaf-monkeys. The existence of any large ape in Burma is doubted.

Insectivora. Among Insectivora may be mentioned shrews of several kinds, two species of gymnura, resembling large shrews, moles, and the very curious flying lemur.

Cheiroptera. Flying foxes and about twenty species of bats, haunting caves, hollow trees, ruined pagodas, and other old buildings are exceedingly common. They dwell in myriads in the caves near Moulmein and at Pāgăt in the Amherst district.

Cetacea. The Irrawaddy porpoise is found in the Irrawaddy as far north as Bhamo, and dolphins in tidal waters.

Edentata. The Malay and Chinese pangolin, or scaly ant-eaters, are specimens of this family.

Birds. Birds are of a myriad species, for a bare catalogue of which space cannot be found. Of game birds, most characteristic of Burma is the snipe which, in the swampy plains of Lower Burma and in irrigated fields elsewhere at the right season, abounds in unparalleled profusion. Over a hundred couple have fallen to a single gun in one day. The pintail and the fantail or common snipe of India are about equally numerous. Cotton or goose teal, not very plentiful, are widely distributed. The blue winged common teal, large and small whistling ducks, pintail, grey duck, pochard, and others frequent meres (jheels). The Brahminy duck keeps generally to sandbanks in rivers; as also does the bar-headed goose; while the grey lag goose is found only on meres and marshes. Many kinds of pheasants, silver, peacock, pie-back, crimson tragopan, Mrs Hume's, Anderson's silver, abound. The gorgeous argus pheasant is very rare. The Chinese francolin, well known by his call—"Have a drink Papa"—is the common partridge of the country; bamboo partridges and other kinds are also found. Pea fowl, jungle fowl, plover, golden and stone as well as others, the Burmese lapwing, familiar for its quaint call—"Did he do it?"—are plentiful. Button quail are widely distributed but not very abundant. Woodcock may be shot in divers places but are somewhat scarce. Doves and pigeons, including imperial and many other species of green pigeon, are common.

Many kinds of waders, sandpipers, stints, and the curlew visit Burma in the winter months.

Of two or three kinds of vultures, the commonest are the white-backed, which in large flocks hover over carrion. Eagles are more rare but some half a dozen varieties have been seen, as well as harriers, goshawks, kites, sparrowhawks, peregrines, kestrels, and ospreys. Cormorants of two or three species are in some abundance. The darter or snake bird is common and pelicans are noted in their season.

Herons, egrets, and bitterns are very abundant, the night heron and the pond heron (paddy bird) being among the best known. Adjutants or gigantic storks usually go in pairs but are sometimes seen in flocks; other species of storks and ibis frequent suitable localities.

Of birds of beautiful plumage may be specified the lovely and charmingly named fairy blue bird; several bulbuls; magpies; bright coloured minivets, including the gorgeous scarlet minivet called by the Burmese the prince bird, *Hnget-mintha*; half a dozen kinds of glowing orioles; the Burmese paradise fly catcher; resplendent sun birds of many species; broadbills; woodpeckers; blue jays; the Burmese night jar; kingfishers. Flocks of gay parroquets fly over fields and forests.

The house-crow, aptly called *Corvus insolens*, is ubiquitous; the jungle crow less abundant. Drongos are common, the best known perhaps being the black drongo or king-crow and the racquet-tailed drongo.

Tits, babblers, nuthatches, warblers of nearly fifty species, and a dozen kinds of shrikes are more or less common.

The Burmese talking myna, the Indian grackle, found all over the Province, is not really a myna. Many starlings and real mynas abound, the most familiar being the common or house myna and the noisy Burmese pied myna. Chats, robins, ground- and rock-thrushes, fork-tails, ouzels and other kindred species, include the pied bush chat, one of the commonest birds in Burma. The magpie-robin, a charming singer, is a familiar bird near houses and villages. Another fine song bird frequenting the forest, rather like a magpie but with a rufous breast, is the shama. Larks of various species including the skylark are seen and heard.

Weaver-birds are of several kinds, some among the best known birds in the country. The house-sparrow and the tree-sparrow flourish everywhere; and many species of swallows and martins, some migrant, others resident, abound.

Swifts of some kinds are numerous. In the islands of the Mergui Archipelago *Collocalia francica*, the little grey-rumped swiftlet, builds the edible bird's nests of commerce.

The hoopoe and the common Indian bee-eater are among the most familiar birds. The great hornbill abounds in all dense forests. A dozen kinds of cuckoo are widely spread. But the note of *Cuculus canorus* is heard only in the hills. Of the same family is the Burmese concal or crow pheasant. Of barbets, only the crimson-breasted, or coppersmith, need be mentioned.

Owls include fish, hawk and barn owls. The Burmese sarus crane is not common or widely distributed. Gulls and tern frequent the coasts. The little grebe or dab-chick may close the list.

Snakes. Snakes of many kinds are unpleasantly and dangerously abundant. Of deadly snakes, the largest and most formidable is the hamadryad (*Naia bungarus*), one of the few savage creatures which sometimes attack and pursue without provocation. There are authentic records of men having been chased by this monster which attains the length of thirteen feet. But ordinarily even the hamadryad does not attack unless provoked or alarmed. The cobra (*N. tripudians*), the lurking krait (*Bungarus coeruleus*), and Russell's viper (*Vipera Russellii*) are also snakes whose poison is almost invariably fatal. *B. coeruleus* is, however, very rare. Its place is taken by *B. fasciatus*, the banded or Burmese krait, fairly common but so inoffensive that Burmans believe it not to be poisonous. It is sometimes called the pôngyi[1] snake from its bright canary, alternating with prune purple, bands, a very distinctive marking. The snake which does most damage and is by far the most numerous and most troublesome is Russell's viper, *mwe-bwe*. So dangerous and plentiful is he in dry districts such as Magwe and Sagaing that, when reaping the fields or walking after dark, the country folk wear special boots, with palm-wood soles and matting or reed uppers, to protect themselves against his attack. They know about the height the snake can strike. Most deadly of all are sea-snakes (*Hydrophidae*) of which several varieties haunt coasts and estuaries. Enormous pythons growing as long as twenty feet are often seen. There are also many kinds of snakes which are quite harmless.

Lizards. Lizards, great and small, of many varieties are found everywhere; in forests and in human habitations. Most interesting is *Gecko verticillatus*, the large *tak-tu*, so called from its strange cry, a popular and almost domesticated reptile. Though of somewhat formidable appearance,

---

[1] The dress of monks (pôngyis) is the yellow robe.

it is quite harmless. It has been seen in successful conflict with a snake, but this must be a rare occurrence. The tak-tu and other lizards or geckos of smaller size frequent houses and are constantly seen clinging to the walls and ceilings of dwelling rooms.

Crocodiles. Crocodiles are found on the sea-coast and in rivers. Three species are distinguished.

Turtles. Four principal kinds of turtle are green (*Chelone mydas*), the edible variety; logger-head; hawk's-bill, yielding the true tortoise-shell of commerce; and leathery. Many other species of turtles and tortoises are also found. The most famous turtle bank is at Diamond Island.

Some of the turtles are four feet long, and all are of a prodigious thickness. It is interesting to see a dark, bulky form, wet and glistening in the moonlight, emerge from the sea and toil slowly up the sloping sands. Active enough in the water, the turtle is a slow heavy mover on land. Laboriously she pushes herself along with her short flappers until she finds a place which satisfies her meticulous, maternal instinct. She scoops out a nest in the sand, some two feet deep, and lays her eggs, a couple of hundred more or less. She then covers them up with sand and leaves them to shift for themselves. It is just as well that that is the last their parent knows about them, for the fate that too frequently befalls them would break an affectionate mother's heart. Generally they are dug up the following morning and despatched to the bazaars for the consumption of Burmese epicures. If a nest is overlooked and the young are hatched they have many other enemies. They run down to the sea as fast as they can, but few reach sanctuary, for cormorants, sea-gulls, and big fish lie in wait to slaughter the innocents[1].

Frogs and toads are of many species. And leeches infest the forests to an incredible extent.

Fishes. Rivers and the sea abound in fish; fisheries are a source of wealth and sustenance to the community and of revenue to the State. The greatest fisheries are those of the Irrawaddy Delta where definite sections of streams and creeks are leased to master fishermen. In these areas, fish

[1] Marjorie Laurie.

are caught by means of weirs and traps fixed in the water. In free river and in sea fisheries, also of considerable importance, fees are levied on nets and fishing implements. On account of the destruction of life involved, the fisherman's occupation is regarded with disfavour by pious Buddhists. But the product of his industry is not rejected or contemned. A great part of the produce of sea and river fisheries is converted into *ngapi*, specially prepared fish paste with an odour rivalling that of the *durian*[1], the most popular condiment with all classes of Burmans.

"*Cyprinidae* and *Siluridae* compose the great mass of fish in the fresh waters and estuaries of Burma[2]." Colonel F. D. Maxwell, who in 1904 prepared an exhaustive report on the Delta fisheries, enumerates fifty-two kinds, the best known being varieties of goby, butter-fish, carp, barbel, perch, mango-fish, mullet, and pomfret. An extremely delicate and fine-flavoured fish is hilsa (*Clupea ilisha*), caught in tidal rivers and, though rarely, in the Irrawaddy as far north as Mandalay. The multitude of its bones is excessive. In the upper reaches of the Irrawaddy, in the 'Nmaikha and Mali-kha, and in hill streams elsewhere, mahseer are abundant. In remote Putao is magnificent mahseer fishing. The record for that district is a fish of 86 lbs.; the record fish for Burma was caught at Myitkyina and weighed 96 lbs. To revert to the sea, sharks are fairly plentiful, but attacks by sharks are comparatively rare.

Off the coast of Mergui, pearling was practised for many years by the Salôn[3]. Since 1893 it has been pursued by modern methods with mediocre success. A good many pearls are found, but the fishing does not rank high among the great pearl fisheries of the world. Other sea-fisheries afford occupation to numbers of fishermen on this coast; the yield being mainly prawns and shrimps for conversion into *ngapi*. Green snails and sea-slugs (*bêche-de-mer*) are gathered and exported to China and the Straits.

---

[1] See p. 145.   [2] Day.   [3] See p. 45.

Insects. Insect life is prodigious and almost spoils an otherwise exquisite land. Mosquitoes, anopheles and others, are endemic and ubiquitous, of great size and ferocity. In the Irrawaddy Delta where, perhaps, they are most abundant, cattle have to be kept under mosquito nets; and European houses are "closed at sunset with mosquitoproof shutters of fine wire gauze." Horseflies are exceedingly troublesome. They seem to have impressed Father Sangermano even more than mosquitoes. Gigantic spiders festoon the forests with their webs and haunt the houses of men; some of extravagantly hideous aspect. Scorpions of many species are common. Cicadas fill the valleys with strident sound. White ants (so called) are universal in their season, destructive of books and furniture and house posts in one stage of their progress, vastly annoying in another stage when they fly in myriads and deposit clouds of wings and masses of pulpy bodies. True ants of many kinds and of interesting habits, including "the notorious and vicious red ant," flourish in great numbers. Beetles, of many species, some of brilliant colouring, some of amazing size, are as the sands of the sea for multitude. Fireflies light up the banks of creeks, among the few bright spots in the insect world. Houseflies, gnats, sand-flies, locusts, cockroaches, crickets, and innumerable other pests, fly or creep, bite or sting, making life almost intolerable, especially in the early rains. The Order *Rhynchota* is widely diffused. One green little flying monster of this Order, probably *Nezara viridula*, has a peculiarly disgusting and persistent odour which clings to all that it touches and defies the perfumes of Araby. Another unmitigated nuisance is the mole cricket (*Gryllotalpa Africana*) which swarms out of the ground in thousands and combines all the unpleasing habits of flying, crawling and biting. Like the hamadryad it charges unprovoked. It climbs to embarrassing heights and to wearers of skirts is a more legitimate cause of terror than a mouse.

CHAPTER XI

HISTORY

LEGENDS and myths, unprofitable to relate, fill the early chronicles of Burma. In times of which there are no authentic records, the Burmese, issuing from the highlands of central Asia, drove into Lower Burma the Talaings, the first inhabitants of whom we have any knowledge, and occupied Upper Burma. They are said to have established a kingdom with its capital at **Tagaung** in the 9th century, B.C.[1]. Early in our era, Shans invaded and overspread the north of Burma and founded a dominion which endured for hundreds of years. The Burmans retreated to **Pagan**, below Myingyan, said to have been built in the 2nd century, A.D.[2]. Thus, for many centuries, in a welter of conflict, Shans dominated the north and east; Burmans held the middle country; Talaings the south, part of which however belonged to Siam. Arakan was independent. These are merely approximate and to some extent conjectural generalizations. It would be vain to assign limits to these kingdoms or dates to events; idle to record the names and exploits of kings celebrated in native chronicles and accumulated legends. Of the Pyu there is nothing definite to record except that they had their capital at Prome up to the time of Anawrata. A few Pyu inscriptions remain.

The five kings worth remembering are Anawrata, Tabin Shweti, Bayin Naung, Alaungpaya and Mindôn Min. Serious history dawns with the reign of **Anawrata** who ruled at Pagan for over forty years (1010–52). This great king extended his sway over the greater part of Burma.

---

[1] At Tagaung, on the left bank of the Irrawaddy in the Katha district, can still be traced remains of a royal city.

[2] Pagan, of which remains exist, dates from 847 A.D.

In the north he broke the Shan dominion, which had already disintegrated into many independent States, and subjugated the country as far as Bhamo[1]. Thatôn and Pegu were taken and the Talaings reduced to subjection. Arakan, which had been invaded and for a few years held by Shans, became tributary. For some two centuries the Pagan kingdom flourished. Marco Polo (1272–90) mentions the King of Mien (Burma) as "a very puissant Prince, with much territory, treasure, and people." But the traveller saw these glories fade, this strength diminish. He describes a battle at Yungchang between the Burmese and Kublai Khan's army. The elephants on which the Burmese chiefly relied were thrown into confusion and put to flight by Tartar bowmen and the troops of the Great Khan won a signal victory. Somewhat later (1284), Pagan itself was taken and sacked and the Burmese kingdom was broken to pieces. The next half century witnessed the rise and fall of two Shan kingdoms, with capitals at Panya and Sagaing respectively, extending as far south as Prome.

In 1364 Burmese supremacy was restored by Thadomin who claimed descent from the ancient kings of Tagaung. He erected his capital at **Ava** and he and his successors conquered much of the country formerly ruled from Pagan, as far south as Prome but not including Pegu. Ava was perpetually embroiled with the Shans who still dominated the north; and for a time Shan kings from Mo-hnyin occupied the throne.

Meanwhile Pegu, after regaining its independence, was overrun by Wareru who had set up a new Talaing kingdom at Martaban which eventually tore Tavoy and Tenasserim from Siam. Later, in 1323, the capital was moved to **Pegu**. In the latter part of the 14th and first part of the 15th century Ava and Pegu were seldom at peace with each other.

[1] The more remote Shan States, such as Mogaung and Mo-hnyin, retained their independence.

Since the downfall of Pagan (1284), the small territory of **Toungoo**, peopled by Burmans, had been practically uncontrolled. But it was not till 1470, nearly two centuries later, that its independence was formally asserted. The first notable event in its history is the accession (1530) of one of the most conspicuous figures in Burmese annals, **Tabin Shweti** (1530–50), who claimed descent from Anawrata. Extending his rule successively over Pegu (1538–39), whither he transferred his capital; Martaban; and Prome (1541–42); he defeated the Shan king of Ava (1544) and occupied his territory as far as Pagan. After his death, for a short time, the power of Pegu declined. It was restored and enhanced by Tabin Shweti's famous general, **Bayin Naung** (1551–81), who, after a short interval, became king. This great soldier and ruler subjugated Ava (1554); finally and effectively broke the Shan dominion (1557–58), as relics whereof in Burma proper only isolated States survived; reduced all the Shan country as far north as China and Assam, as far east as Chieng mai[1]; and ruled over the whole of Burma except Arakan and presumably the remote hill tracts. Siam was twice invaded, Ayuthia taken (1563–64), and three white elephants, the ostensible object of the first expedition, carried off (1568–69). Bayin Naung's tempestuous glorious reign ended as he was planning operations against Arakan (1581). This was the brightest epoch of Burmese civilization. Cæsar Frederick, whose description of Pegu (1569) is given elsewhere[2], writes of Bayin Naung:

There is not a King on the earth that has more power or strength than the King of Pegu, because he has twenty and six Kings at his command. He can make in his camp a million and a half of men of warre in the field against his enemies....This King of Pegu hath not any army or power by sea, but in the land, for people, dominions, gold and silver, he far exceeds the power of the great Turke in treasure and strength....Also he is Lord of the Mines of Rubies, Sapphires, and Spinels[3].

[1] Now subject to Siam.   [2] p. 182.   [3] Hakluyt, II. 365.

Doubtless this report inspired Butler's reference to the Burmese king[1].

After Bayin Naung the glory waned. Siam became independent. Pegu was taken and destroyed by invaders from Toungoo and Arakan (1599), and a Talaing king was set up at Martaban. By degrees the empire was partly restored and a king again ruled in Pegu (1634). Some years later the capital was transferred to Ava. In the next hundred years, under feeble rulers, outlying districts were lost and disastrous wars were waged with China and with Manipur. Finally, assisted by Shans settled in Pegu (called by the Burmese Gwè Shans), the Talaings rebelled (1740). They occupied Toungoo and Prome and, after some years of desultory fighting, captured and burnt Ava and put an end to the dynasty of Bayin Naung (1752).

Fig. 42. Burmese official (old style).

The ascendancy of the Talaings was of brief duration. Immediately after the fall of Ava, revolt was initiated by a petty official, afterwards known as Aungzeya, the Victorious, and even more widely renowned as **Alaungpaya**. His rise was more swift and miraculous than Napoleon's. Early in 1752 he was a village headman. Before the end of 1753 he was proclaimed king, received the submission of the northern Shan chiefs,

[1] "Grave as the Emperor of Pegu." *Hudibras*, I. ii. 155.

established his capital at his native village, Shwebo, and occupied the royal city of Ava. Continuing the war with the Talaings, Alaungpaya advanced as far as the Shwe Dagôn pagoda (1755), near which he laid out a new city and called it **Rangoon**; took Syriam, the port of Pegu and seat of European trade (1756); and in the year of the battle of Plassey occupied Pegu (1757). By this time his rule extended over the whole of Burma except Arakan. Siam was next invaded (1760) and Ayuthia invested. But sickness forced Alaungpaya to retreat, and before he reached the Salween the great conqueror was dead. A contemporary account[1] describes him as of impressive personality and overweening arrogance. Beyond doubt his name is notable in the world's history.

Ten kings of Alaungpaya's race succeeded him:

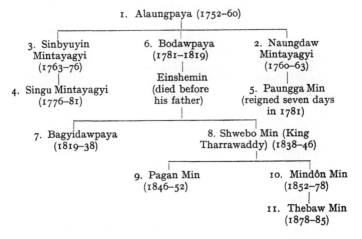

1. Alaungpaya (1752–60)

3. Sinbyuyin Mintayagyi (1763–76)

4. Singu Mintayagyi (1776–81)

6. Bodawpaya (1781–1819)

Einshemin (died before his father)

2. Naungdaw Mintayagyi (1760–63)

5. Paungga Min (reigned seven days in 1781)

7. Bagyidawpaya (1819–38)

8. Shwebo Min (King Tharrawaddy) (1838–46)

9. Pagan Min (1846–52)

10. Mindôn Min (1852–78)

11. Thebaw Min (1878–85)

Sinbyuyin successfully repelled two formidable Chinese invasions, annexed Manipur, and in war with Siam once more destroyed Ayuthia. Bodawpaya conquered Arakan (1784) and brought across the hills the famous statue of

---

[1] By Captain Robert Baker, sent as an envoy by the East India Company in 1755.

Gaudama Buddha, which still stands at Mandalay in the Arakan pagoda[1]. His successor, Bagyidaw, annexed Assam (1821). This year saw the height of Burmese prosperity under the House of Alaungpaya.

Soon afterwards, Burmese incursions into Chittagong brought about a conflict with the Indian Government and caused the **First Burmese War** (1824). The Burmans put up a stout resistance. Rangoon was occupied by General

Fig. 43. Burmese cannon.

Sir Archibald Campbell about the middle of 1824. Later in the year a large force under Maha Bandula made a determined but unsuccessful attack on the town and suburbs. Next year (1825), two British columns moved up the river and Bandula was defeated and slain at Danubyu. The war was ended by a Treaty concluded at Yandabo, not far below Ava, by which Assam, Manipur, Arakan and

[1] This image is said to have been cast in the reign of Chanda Surya, King of Arakan, who came to the throne in 146 A.D.

Tenasserim were ceded by the Burmese (1826). A quarter of a century later Burmese oppression of English traders occasioned the **Second War** (1852). The resistance offered by the Burmese was far less strenuous than in the First War; and General Godwin occupied Pegu and all the country as far as Myedè before the close of the year[1]. By proclamation of the Governor-General, all the territory south of a line drawn east and west, six miles north of Myedè was annexed. Stone pillars marking the boundary were erected, those on the banks of the Irrawaddy under the personal supervision of Lord Dalhousie. Mindôn Min declined to sign away any part of his kingdom and no treaty was concluded. But British occupation was not challenged.

Friendly relations were maintained throughout the reign of **Mindôn Min**, an astute and in some ways enlightened monarch, of whom Sir Henry Yule wrote[2]:

The King is, without doubt, a remarkable man for a Burman; but rather in moral than in intellectual character, though his intelligence, also, is above the average....The Sovereign of Burma is just and mild in temper, easy of access, hears or seeks to hear everything for himself, is heartily desirous that his subjects shall not be oppressed, and strives to secure their happiness....As long as he lives and reigns, peace will probably be maintained.

This prediction was fulfilled. But in the nerveless hands of Mindôn Min's successor authority slackened and anarchy supervened. After the massacre of many members of the Royal Family, for seven years **King Thebaw** and his Ministers allowed Upper Burma to become the prey of dacoits and corrupt officials. Finally misrule, oppression of British traders, and attempts at intrigues with European powers, forced on the **Third War** (1885). King Thebaw had no standing army, no munitions of war, no money in

[1] Ensign Wolseley served in this war and was wounded at Danubyu.
[2] The Court of Ava.

his Treasury. With unprecedented celerity, a small but well-equipped force of 10,000 men under General Sir Harry Prendergast, V.C., crossed the frontier on 14th November; and after one not very serious encounter at Minhla, occupied Mandalay within a fortnight. The king and queen surrendered and were sent to India where they remained

Fig. 44. Summer-house where King Thebaw surrendered.

till Thebaw's death, a few years ago. The remnant of the Burmese kingdom was annexed and Burma once more became an undivided nation.

The pacification[1] occupied the next four or five years. At the outset Upper Burma was in a state of anarchy. Dacoit[2] bands infested the country-side. Chinese brigands

[1] See Sir Charles Crosthwaite's book, *The Pacification of Burma*.
[2] Technically, a dacoit is one of a body of five or more banded together for purposes of robbery.

penetrated as far as Bhamo. The Shan States were in revolt. Hill men raided the plains and levied toll on caravans. Gradually order was established in the plains (1890). The Shan country was more easily brought to submission (1887), most of the chiefs accepting office and continuing in charge of their States. The names associated with the settlement of the Shans are those of Mr A. H. Hildebrand and Sir George Scott. Eastern Karenni was subdued (1889); its turbulent chief, Sawlapaw, fled and was replaced by his nephew Sawlawi, who proved a capable and loyal ruler. The Chin Hills were not finally dominated till after operations lasting for four years (1888–91). For nearly six years (1888–93) fighting continued in the Kachin Hills. The Chins gave some trouble recently; but order has been restored.

Of the distinguished men who took part in the conquest and pacification of Upper Burma may be mentioned, besides Sir Harry Prendergast, Lord Dufferin, who, as Governor-General, visited Mandalay and decreed the annexation; Lord Roberts, who, as Commander-in-Chief, spent some time in Burma directing military operations; Sir Charles Bernard, Chief Commissioner 1885–87; Sir Charles Crosthwaite, from 1887–90; Sir Herbert Macpherson, Commander-in-Chief of the Madras army, who died in Burma; and Sir Charles Arbuthnot who succeeded him; Sir George White[1] who commanded the forces for several years; Sir William Penn Symons who did admirable work in the plains and also in the Chin Hills; Sir Edward Stedman, organizer of the military police; Sir James Willcocks who spent in the Province some months of his early service.

Early travellers. After Marco Polo (1272–90), who may possibly have visited Burma, the earliest known European in the country was Nicolo di Conti, a Venetian, who travelled in Arakan and Ava (1430). Some years later

---

[1] Afterward Commander-in-Chief in India and later the defender of Ladysmith.

(1496), Hieronymo da Santo Stephano, a Genoese, and
Ludovico Bartlema of Bologna, came to Pegu. The first
Portuguese was Ruy Nunez d'Acunha, early in the 16th
century. Next came the reputed liar[1], Fernan Mendez
Pinto, who says he was at sieges of Martaban and Prome
and mentions the well-known names of Dalla (opposite
Rangoon), Dagôn (the great pagoda), Danubyu, Henzada,
and Myedè. Later in the 16th century, Cæsar Frederick,
a Venetian merchant (1569), and Ralph Fitch (1586), the
first Englishman in Burma, came to Pegu and have left
valuable records of their journeys.

Relations with European countries. The Portuguese,
the earliest European settlers, established factories at Martaban and Syriam. Later (1519), Dutch settlements were
founded at Syriam, Negrais and even as far north as Bhamo.
Early in the 17th century, the British East India Company
began to trade regularly with Burma and in process of
time set up agencies at Syriam, Prome, Ava and Bhamo.
British merchants settled also at Mergui, then a Siamese
port. In the first years of the 17th century the Portuguese
were expelled and somewhat later all other foreigners were
driven out. The Portuguese and Dutch did not return. But
at the close of the century British factories were again
established at Syriam, Bassein and Negrais. The French
also had an agency at Syriam till they were evicted by
Alaungpaya. The British factory at Negrais was destroyed
in 1759; but was rebuilt two years later. From that time,
the East India Company maintained uninterrupted commercial relations with Burma.

When first annexed (1826) the Divisions of Arakan and
Tenasserim were administered by Commissioners. The Pegu
Division was constituted after the Second War (1853). Some
years later (1862) these three Divisions were amalgamated
into the Province of British Burma, the first Chief Commissioner being Sir Arthur Phayre, one of the most distin-

---

[1] Congreve.

guished of British administrators. After the Third War the whole of Burma was formed into a Province (1886); and in 1897, Sir Frederic Fryer became the first Lieutenant-Governor.

Many towns have been mentioned as capitals of the whole kingdom or of various parts. The House of Alaung-paya adopted the custom of moving the capital whenever the throne was occupied except by regular succession. The capitals of the several kings of that dynasty were:

Alaungpaya	Shwebo	Bodawpaya	Amarapura
Naungdaw	Sagaing	Bagyidaw	Ava
Sinbyuyin		Shwebo Min	
Singu Min	Ava	Pagan Min	Amarapura
Paungga Min		Mindôn Min	
		Thebaw Min	Mandalay

Those kings who did not change their capital were all deposed.

CHAPTER XII

ADMINISTRATION

THE administration of Burma as a Province of the Indian Empire is in a state of transition. The facts as they stand must be recorded. But it should be remembered that, following the new constitution which will be adopted in the near future, some changes will be introduced in the existing system.

Civil. At the head of the administration is the Lieutenant-Governor, directly responsible to the Government of India and exercising all the powers of a Local Government, controlling all departments of the public service except purely imperial branches, military, post and telegraphs. At present there is no Executive Council. The Legislative Council is composed (July 1922) of 29 members, exclusive of the Lieutenant-Governor, of whom 13 are officials. Of the non-official members, two are elected, by the Burma Chamber of Commerce and the Rangoon Trades Association respectively. The rest, official and non-official, are appointed by the Local Government with the approval of the Government of India. Among the non-official members are nine Burmans, one Chinese, one Karen, one Mahomedan, and one Parsi. The Council enacts laws applicable to the whole or any part of the Province, the Shan States included. Members have the right of asking questions, of moving resolutions, and of discussing the budget. Laws passed by the Council require the assent of the Lieutenant-Governor and of the Governor-General.

Under the new constitution about to be established the Lieutenant-Governor will become Governor; the Legislative Council will consist of 92 members of whom 60 per cent. will be elected, and will have wide powers of controlling the administration; the system of dyarchy will be introduced. An Executive Council and responsible Ministers will be appointed; some branches will be administered by the Governor in Council, the rest by the Governor on the advice of his Ministers.

Upper Burma, exclusive of the Shan States, is a Scheduled District, that is, a territory for which the Governor-General has power to make Regulations without the aid or intervention of a legislative body. In the early years after the annexation, this power was freely exercised; but since the establishment of a local Legislative Council it is seldom needed. The law administered in other parts of India prevails, generally, in Lower Burma. As in other Provinces, there are local systems of land and revenue administration and there is a special Village Law. Upper Burma, less sophisticated, enjoys many modifications and simplifications of the general law applicable to British India. This privilege is unlikely to endure.

The Province is parcelled into eight Divisions, each under a Commissioner; Pegu, Irrawaddy, Arakan, and Tenasserim with headquarters at Rangoon, Bassein, Akyab and Moulmein, respectively; and in Upper Burma, Mandalay, Sagaing, Meiktila and Magwe, each named after its headquarter station[1]. The Commissioner controls all branches of the administration under the Local Government; in Upper Burma and in Arakan, he is also Sessions Judge.

There are 38 districts grouped as shown below:

Division	District	Division	District
Pegu	Rangoon	Irrawaddy	Bassein
	Hanthawaddy.		Ma-u-bin
	(Rangoon)[2]		Pyapôn
	Insein		Henzada
	Tharrawaddy		Myaung-mya
	Pegu		

[1] Rearrangement of Divisions is in contemplation. See Appendix II.
[2] Except where indicated in brackets, each district takes its name from its headquarter station.

Division	District	Division	District
Arakan	Akyab Kyaukpyu Sandoway Hill District of Arakan (Paletwa)	Sagaing	Sagaing Shwebo Lower Chindwin (Môn-ywa) Upper Chindwin (Maw-laik) Chin Hills (Falam)
Tenasserim	Amherst (Moulmein) Thatôn Toungoo Tavoy Mergui Salween (Papun)	Meiktila	Meiktila Myingyan Yamèthin Kyauksè
Mandalay	Mandalay Katha[1] Bhamo Myitkyina Putao (Fort Hertz)[2]	Magwe	Magwe Minbu Pakôkku Thayetmyo

Each district is in charge of a Deputy Commissioner, who administers all except the imperial departments. Here again it must be noted that changes are impending which will seriously reduce the powers of the Deputy Commissioner. But in this sketch, the state actually existing must be described. In respect of public works, education, forests and medical affairs, the Deputy Commissioner's control is general and does not involve interference in technical matters of detail. He is Collector and District Magistrate. Except in the Arakan Hill Tracts and Salween, where a police officer holds charge, he is always a member of what is known as the Burma Commission or of the Burma Civil Service. The Commission consists of Indian Civilians, officers of the Indian army in civil employ, and officers belonging to neither of these services but individually appointed with the sanction of the Secretary of State, or selected by the Local Government from the Burma Civil Service. The last-named service was formerly called the Provincial Civil Service. It consists for the most part of

[1] The Ruby Mines, formerly a separate district with headquarters at Mogôk, has been merged into Katha.
[2] Named after Mr W. A. Hertz, the first Deputy Commissioner.

Burmese officers. The employment of Burmans in charges of responsibility has been much extended in recent years. In 1908, the first tentative appointment of a Burman (really an Arakanese) to the charge of a light district was hazarded. In July, 1921, four districts were in charge of Burmans, including two important Lower Burma districts[1].

Quite recently (1922) District Councils and Circle Boards

Fig. 45. At the well.

have been established in most districts, for the purpose of educating the mass of the people in self-government. Circle Boards control groups of village tracts; their members are elected by popular vote, women having the franchise. Members of District Councils are elected by Circle Boards. Officials are not eligible for seats in either of these assemblies; and official interference is jealously excluded. These Councils and Boards are to administer vernacular education, vaccination, hospitals, markets, veterinary dis-

[1] In July, 1922, there were only two Burmese Deputy Commissioners.

pensaries, slaughter-houses, sanitation, roads, and waterways. They will impose taxation for local purposes.

Most districts are partitioned into sub-divisions and these
again into townships. Many of the sub-divisional and practically all the township officers (Myo-ôks) are natives of

Fig. 46. A Myo-thugyi.

the country, the great majority of Burmese race. Formerly
there was a further territorial division; in Lower Burma,
the circle (*taik*), in Upper Burma, the *myo*, each an aggregate of village areas under a *Taik-thugyi* or a *Myo-thugyi*
respectively. These have for the most part disappeared,
and the territorial unit is now the village. Consistent
efforts have been made to preserve and strengthen the

village organization. Every village has its Headman, appointed by the Deputy Commissioner from among the villagers. In the making of this appointment, so far as possible, regard is paid to hereditary claims and also to the wishes of the people. The Headman is the leading villager; the village magistrate and judge, with power to try petty criminal and civil cases, and the local revenue collector. The elders have no legal power or status, but in practice they exercise substantial influence. All villagers are bound by law to assist the headman in the discharge of his public duties; and new comers cannot settle in a village without his permission. On all residents is imposed joint responsibility for peace and order. They are bound to keep the village in a state of defence and to resist armed attack. If an undetected crime is committed, or if stolen property is traced to its borders, the village is held responsible.

The Shan States are administered on special lines[1]. The Shan plateau, occupying an area of over fifty thousand square miles, is distributed into a number of States varying in size from a few acres to thousands of square miles, each under its hereditary Chief. In the later times of Burmese rule, the Chiefs were constantly fighting one another and a country once prosperous was laid waste. Since our coming, peace has been restored and excellent progress has been made. The States are grouped into two main sections, the Southern, with headquarters at Taung-gyi, the Northern, with headquarters at Lashio, each under a Superintendent. These States are an integral part of British India, as they were formerly of the Burmese kingdom, and are not on the footing of native States in other parts of India. The form of administration which prevailed under Burmese rule has been preserved; and each State is governed by its own Chief, entitled *Sawbwa*, *Myosa*, or *Ngwe-kun-hmu*. The Imperial and Provincial[2] Legislatures enact laws applicable

[1] See Appendix IV.
[2] Apparently the Provincial Legislature will no longer enact laws for the Shan States.

to these States; and the enlightened Chief of Yawnghwe was long a member of the Provincial Legislative Council. The internal affairs of each State are administered by the Chief, subject to the supervision and guidance of the Superintendents and their assistants. Gradually the Chiefs have learnt to administer their revenues with care and to take an interest in public works and other measures for the benefit of their people. A good school for the sons of Chiefs and notables flourishes at Taung-gyi. Modified by rules to prohibit cruel and barbarous practices and to prescribe a simple judicial procedure, the customary law remains in force. Government reserves all rights to forests and minerals and regulates the relations between the several States. Order is maintained by comparatively small bodies of military police and there are a few civil police. But the Chiefs are responsible for peace and order in their own territories. The succession to any Chief is subject to the approval of government. Each Chief on his accession receives a Sanad or Order of appointment defining his rights and privileges and prescribing his duties and limitations. The principal States are Kēngtūng, an extensive territory east of the Salween; Yawnghwe, a western State, wherein is situate the headquarters of the southern section; Möngnai, to the east, but cis-Salween; Hsipaw and North and South Hsenwi in the northern group[1].

Outside of the main sections are two other Shan States, sole relics of Shan predominance in Upper Burma; Hsawnghsup (Thaungthut) and Singaling Hkampti, both on the Chindwin subject to the Commissioner of Sagaing. Hkampti Lōng, in the far north, is now practically part of the Putao district. Möngmit, formerly under the Commissioner of Mandalay, has lately been attached to the Northern Shan States. The old States of Kale and Wuntho were absorbed long ago into Upper Chindwin and Katha respectively.

Karenni, which lies to the north-east of Lower Burma,

[1] For a complete list of the Shan States, see Appendix III.

between 18° and 20° N. and 97° and 99° E. with an area of 7200 square miles, intersected by the Salween, consists of a group of feudatory States, not an integral part of the Province. It is administered, much on the lines of the Shan States, by several Chiefs, mutually independent, with the advice of an Assistant Superintendent stationed at Loikaw and subordinate to the Superintendent of the Southern Shan States.

The Chin Hills on the north-west, adjoining Assam, Manipur and Chittagong, are administered as a district of the Sagaing division by a Deputy Commissioner whose headquarters are at Falam, with assistants at Tiddim, Haka and Lotaw. The Chin chiefs, headmen of villages and groups of villages, enjoy a large measure of independence and there is as little interference as possible with local customs. The laws in force are provided by Regulation and other legislative enactment. The Pakôkku Hill Tracts to the south, under the control of a Superintendent with head-quarters at Kanpetlet near Mt Victoria, form part of the Magwe division.

The Kachin Hills on the north-east and north are in-cluded in the Bhamo, Myitkyina and Putao districts. Here also villages and groups of villages are controlled by head-men (*Duwa*). As much regard as possible is paid to local customs and the ordinary law is modified by Regulation to adapt it to the backward condition of these tracts.

To return to the settled districts of the Province, justice, civil and criminal, is administered under the control of the Chief Court in Lower Burma and of the Judicial Commis-sioner in Upper Burma[1]. Till the year 1900, a Judicial Commissioner was the head of the judicial administration in Lower Burma. In that year, the Chief Court was estab-lished, consisting of a Chief Judge and Judges of whom one half at least must be barristers; all are appointed by the Governor-General in Council. One of the puisne judges is a

---

[1] A High Court for the whole Province has recently been established.

Burman. This Court exercises all the powers of a High Court and controls and supervises all branches of the judicial system. It also tries all cases committed for trial by Sessions or High Court in the town of Rangoon and exercises exclusive jurisdiction over European British subjects throughout the province. With this last-mentioned exception, in Upper Burma the Judicial Commissioner exercises all the powers of a High Court. His sway does not extend over the Shan States or the Kachin and Chin Hills, where the highest judicial authorities are the Superintendents and Commissioners respectively. Officers of the Commission in the regular line usually exercise judicial as well as executive powers, as do many members of the Burma and Subordinate Civil Services. But there are separate services, composed of divisional, sessions, district, sub-divisional, and township judges, whose functions are purely judicial. The bulk of the original judicial work is done by Burmese magistrates and judges.

Police. Law and order are maintained by military and civil police under an Inspector-General with several Deputies. The military police were constituted after the annexation of Upper Burma, being enlisted from the martial races of India. Their duties are the maintenance of order, the custody of the frontiers, the domination of turbulent tribes; they have no concern with the detection of crime. Besides Indians, Kachins, Chins, Karens, and more recently Burmans, have been enrolled in the military police. They are officered by Battalion Commandants and Assistant Commandants, temporarily seconded from the Indian army. From time to time, battalions of military police have been converted into regular regiments.

The civil police consists almost entirely of natives of the Province chiefly under European senior officers. Their duties are the prevention and detection of crime and the prosecution of criminals. In recent years, natives of the Province have been placed in charge of the police of several districts.

Education. The important branch of education is administered by a Department under a Director of Public Instruction. As elsewhere indicated, the basis of primary education of boys is the monastic school system. Besides monastic schools, there are many others, some supported from municipal and town funds, others by missions or private teachers, very few directly by Government. Most schools receive grants in aid from provincial funds, subject to inspection and observance of prescribed courses of study. While elementary education is very widely spread, higher education is in a backward state. Till recently, colleges in Burma were affiliated to the Calcutta University. In 1920, the University of Rangoon was established, consisting of University College, maintained by Government, and Judson College, maintained by the American Baptist Mission Union.

Fig. 47. A modern school-boy.

Municipal. Municipal administration was introduced in 1874 and has since, from time to time, been largely extended. At present there are in Lower Burma 35, and in Upper Burma 13, municipal towns. Many members of municipal committees are elected and in some towns there are non-official presidents and vice-presidents. The tendency is to minimize official control and guidance. In 23 smaller towns committees with somewhat less extensive powers manage local affairs.

Revenue System. Commissioners, deputy commissioners, sub-divisional and township officers, and village headmen are concerned in the revenue administration. At the head is the Financial Commissioner. In Lower Burma, the land revenue system is comparatively simple. The State is the ultimate owner of all culturable land and levies revenue upon it. Private persons hold by grant or lease from Government or by occupation. Any person who occupies culturable land, paying revenue in respect of it, for a continuous period of twelve years, acquires a permanent heritable and transferable title called landholder's right. In practice, though not theoretically, this is indistinguishable from freehold tenure. A good deal of land is

Fig. 48. A village school.

cultivated by tenants under landlords, many of whom are not natives of the Province. The number of large grants is comparatively small. Revenue is levied at varying rates on all culturable land which produces a crop. The rates are fixed at intervals generally of fifteen years by settlement officers who, after elaborate enquiries, propose for the sanction of government rates per acre on land under rice and other cultivation. If land is left fallow, a nominal rate of two annas (3*d*.) an acre is imposed. The State is a liberal landlord. If crops fail, wholly or in part, remission of revenue is freely given after inspection and enquiry.

In Upper Burma the system is more complex. Here, as in Lower Burma, the intention has been to maintain the customs existing under Burmese rule. The two main divisions of land are into State (*lèdaw*) and hereditary (*bobabaing*). *Lèdaw* is the property of the State and is leased to cultivators. Under this head are grouped many tenures of interest, service (*ahmudan*) and others. In Magwe, Katha and Bhamo, communal tenures still subsist. In these cases, all culturable land in a village tract is held in common and is assigned temporarily to individuals, the distribution being in the hands of the headman. If a man has more land than he can properly cultivate, the headman may resume part and allot it to another. *Bobabaing* land is theoretically the private property of individual cultivators and formerly was subject to no State dues. It is now liable to revenue assessment, subject to adjustment of *thathameda*[1].

Land revenue is collected by village headmen who receive a commission on the collections. In 1919–20, the gross land revenue amounted to £3,037,600.

The next great head of revenue in Lower Burma is the capitation tax. This is a poll tax levied at a fixed rate on all adult males. The normal rate is 5s. a year on bachelors and 10s. on married men. Government servants, monks, schoolmasters, and the aged and infirm, are exempt. In poor districts, the rates are reduced. In 1919–20, the receipts were £555,300. In recent years, income tax has been imposed in Lower Burma; payers of income tax do not pay capitation tax. In this way, the obvious inequity of the uniform capitation tax has been remedied.

The corresponding levy in Upper Burma is an impost inherited from native rule called *thathameda*, a graduated income tax. It is levied at varying rates, the highest being

[1] See below.

£1 yearly on each household in a town or village. The rate
having been fixed, the gross amount due from any unit is
the rate multiplied by the number of households. But every
household does not pay at the average rate. The distribution of the assessment is made by a committee of elders
(*thamadi*) who apportion payments according to the means
of the tax-payers. This is a very fair and simple arrange-
ment which, subject to supervision by district officers to
prevent malpractices, works well. In 1919–20, the receipts
from *thathameda* amounted to £400,000.

Opium and Excise. A substantial revenue, in 1921–22
about £1,000,000, is derived from the sale of opium and from
excise duties on alcoholic liquor. It has long been recognized
that for Burmans opium is exceedingly deleterious and de-
moralizing. The opinion of the better classes condemns its
consumption utterly and without reserve. They regard the
use of opium in any form as contrary to the teaching of
their religion and as destructive of the body and soul of
the consumer. For at least fifty years, the policy of Government has been to discourage the use of opium without any
reference to the effect of its disuse on the revenue. But the
problem is not so simple as it might appear and cannot be
solved by a bare prohibition such as is theoretically in force
in China. Many Burmans, many Indians, many Chinese,
many Shans and hillmen, have long been habitual consumers; all except Burmans without obviously ill effects.
To deprive all these of the drug to which they have become
accustomed would be a very drastic measure involving
widespread hardship and distress. Moreover, opium is
easily concealed and transported and the smuggling of
small quantities is a simple process. To enforce absolute
prohibition would necessitate the appointment of an army
of preventive officers. Faced with these difficulties, from
time to time Government has adopted many expedients
for limiting facilities for procuring opium, for raising its
cost, and for preventing illicit traffic. The number of shops

is strictly limited, as well as the quantity allowed to be sold to any individual. In Upper Burma, in accordance with what is believed to have been the rule in the king's time, no Burman is allowed to possess opium. In Lower Burma, only those Burmans may possess it who are registered as consumers. Other races are less severely restricted in all parts of the Province.

The excise administration is based on similar principles. Burmans are discouraged by their religion from drinking intoxicating liquors; but the habit of drinking seems to be increasing. Shops for the sale of liquors are licensed on payment of annual fees. No new shop can be established till the opinion of the people of the locality has been ascertained. As much as is possible in a free country is done to reduce the facilities for obtaining intoxicating drink and to enhance the price.

Customs. As in other Provinces, customs duties for revenue purposes are levied on imports of every description. There is also an export duty on all rice exported elsewhere than to India at the rate of 3d. a maund (about 80 lbs.). Economically, this duty appears to fall on the land and appreciably to raise the incidence of taxation on rice-producing areas. In 1921–22, the net receipts from Customs amounted to £2,870,000.

Fisheries and forests have already been mentioned. In 1919–20, the fishery revenue was £360,000.

Other branches of administration are the Jail Department and the Civil Medical Service. Hospitals and dispensaries are not maintained by private charity but are supported by the State or from municipal and town funds. The first hospital was established in 1826 at Akyab. In 1865, there were 13 hospitals and dispensaries; in 1880, 20; in 1890, 74; in 1900, 113; in 1910, 259; in 1921, 278. In 1865, Government spent on these institutions about £1800. Last year, the expenditure amounted to £260,000, contributed nearly equally by Provincial and by Municipal and other local funds. In 1865, 3000 in and 20,000 out patients were treated. Last year the total number of patients was 1,900,000, of whom 1,200,000 were Burmans and over 57,000 operations were performed. Lately the Department of Public Health, under a Director, has replaced the Sanitary Department. There is a competent Veterinary Department. The Co-operative Credit movement has been brilliantly successful in promoting thrift and economy. In the year 1919–20, there were 4394 societies with 108,868 members.

Among comparatively new appointments may be mentioned the Development Commissioner and the Director of Industries, whose duties are indicated by their titles. The invaluable Agricultural Department has been briefly described in another chapter.

Finance. Revenue and expenditure are distributed between central, provincial, and local funds. In the last-mentioned are included municipal and district funds with others of less note. In 1920–21, the gross revenue of the province was £14,642,300, the expenditure £9,318,300. For the year 1921–22 the income was estimated at £16,039,000, expenditure at £11,886,300. Central receipts were expected to be £5,886,600, outlay £1,020,000. For provincial funds, the budget figures were: income £10,152,400, expenditure £10,866,300. For many years complaints were persistent that the province was badly treated in the financial arrangements imposed by the Government of India. Recently, a new and more liberal settlement has been made, and it is hoped that in future sufficient funds will be available for the proper supply of provincial needs and the due development of provincial resources.

CHAPTER XIII

(I) THE PEOPLE

ACCORDING to the preliminary figures of the census of 1921, the population of the province is 13,204,760, about a million more than in 1911. The increase is common to all districts except Prome, Magwe, and the Chin Hills.

Burmese. Inclusive of Arakanese and some minor classes, Burmese in 1911[1] numbered nearly 8,000,000, or about 66 per cent. of the total population. They predominate in the whole province except the Shan States, the Kachin and Chin Hills, and Karenni. Of their character, manners and customs so much has been written[2] that a detailed description would be superfluous. But a sketch must be given.

Among Burmans, there is no caste and there are few class distinctions. There are no privileged orders, except perhaps officials, no landed aristocracy, no hereditary superiors. Social distinctions, based on wealth and dignity, do not exist. The comparative thinness of population and the fertility of the soil in large areas prevent any serious pressure on subsistence. If there are no great fortunes, there is no grinding poverty.

Physically, short in stature but sturdy and muscular, with a strong superficial resemblance to the Gurkha, the Burman in daily life is high-spirited, reckless, of a gay and boisterous humour. Delighting in fine clothes, in *pwès* (theatrical and other shows), pony races, boat races, and pagoda festivals, he is at heart a gambler and bets on anything. It is told that a Buddhist ecclesiastic came to settle

---

[1] Details of the 1921 census not being yet available, except where otherwise stated the figures in this chapter are those of the census of 1911.

[2] *The Burman*, by Shwe Yoe (Sir George Scott), is still the classical authority.

a serious religious dispute but declined to give a decision when he found that the whole town was wagering on the event[1]. When necessary, Burmans work hard enough, but they have no desire to work for the sake of working or to amass riches. Their standard of living is reasonably high. Their manners are really distinguished. The natural Burman is of a singularly humane disposition. "Kindness to

Fig. 49. Burmese boxing.

strangers is equally the precept and the practice of Burmans[2]." Good treatment of animals is another pleasing trait. One result is seen in the excellent sleekness of Burmese oxen. Children are indulged and in return respect their parents.

Women are not secluded but may be seen in their houses, in the fields, in the streets, by the village well. Girls marry at a reasonable age and to please themselves. Polygamy is allowed and practised, but is by no means universal.

[1] *The Burman.*
[2] Symes, 240.

Divorce is easy and open to each sex on the same terms. Most of the petty trade is carried on by women in bazaars and markets. "Women take part in all agricultural operations; they sow, transplant, reap, carry sheaves, thresh, winnow, and in exceptional cases even plough and cut weeds[1]." As they may not enter monastic schools, all women do not receive elementary education. But more are literate than among most other eastern races. Now that

Fig. 50. Monks.

representative institutions are to be established, it is understood that women will have the vote from the outset. They are as well qualified as men to enjoy this privilege. Burmese women commit practically no serious crimes. Their moral standard is high.

In religion, Burmans are strict Buddhists, though many traces of animism survive. Every village has its pagoda, its monastery (*kyaung*), its rest house (*zayat*) for travellers and pilgrims. The monastic Order is elaborately organized.

[1] *Myaungmya Settlement Report.*

At its head is the *Thathanabaing*[1]; under him in succession *gaing-ôk*, *gaing-dauk*, and heads of monasteries. Monks, of whom there are perhaps a quarter of a million, are supported by voluntary offerings of the faithful, and are bound by vows of poverty and chastity, which are not irrevocable but may be renounced at any time. They exercise no sacerdotal functions; there is no such person as a Buddhist *priest*. They spend their lives in meditation, in the study and exposition of the scriptures, and in teaching young boys. Buddhist nuns are equally respectable but less numerous and conspicuous. They dwell apart in isolation, not in convents. While ordinary Burmans are buried, monks of special sanctity are cremated with much ceremony.

Every small Burman boy passes some time in a monastery even if he has no intention of becoming a monk. There he is taught to read and write and do simple sums; he also receives religious and moral instruction. The initiation of a boy as a neophyte is celebrated with such splendour as his family can afford, in a manner practised without material change for many centuries.

In theory **Buddhism** seems a gloomy religion. Every year nearly three months from July to October are set aside as *Wa* or Lent, when monks and laymen are expected to practise special abstinence and austerity. Every eighth day throughout the year is a day of rest and meditation when monasteries and pagoda platforms are crowded and sermons are preached by fervent monks. A Buddhist is not an idolater. He worships neither the pagoda nor the image of Buddha. These merely help to fix his mind on the Buddha, the Law, and the Assembly. Telling the beads of his rosary, he recites the formula, change, pain, illusion. But he does not pray to any sentient or personal Deity. The ethics of Buddhism are as high and pure as those of any philosophy or creed.

[1] His jurisdiction at present extends only over Upper Burma.

Apart from Buddhism and in strictness discountenanced by it is the prevalent practice of *nat* worship. *Nats* are of two kinds, (1) the inhabitants of the six inferior heavens, the "dewahs" of Hindu mythology; (2) spirits of nature, the house, the air, the water, the forest[1]. It is *nats* of the second class who must be propitiated by offerings and observances.

Burmans are as much addicted to crime as most people. They are sudden and quick in quarrel and the use of knives is deplorably common. Murders and crimes of violence, dacoity, robbery, and cattle theft are prevalent; and dacoits and robbers often treat their victims with revolting barbarity. The standard of veracity and of commercial morality is not so high as could be wished. Nor are the public services yet free from the taint of corruption, a heritage of Burmese rule. In the past, Burmans have been flighty and unstable, impatient of discipline and restraint.

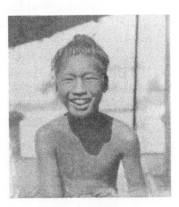

Fig. 51. Jungle boy.

Hence they have not been good soldiers or even good policemen. During the Great War, renewed attempts were made to foster a military spirit. Regiments of Burmans were raised and for the first time Burmans were enlisted in the military police. The Burmese regiments served with credit. But it is too soon to estimate the success of the experiment.

Owing to the custom of sending every boy for a time to a monastery, elementary education is more widely spread in Burma than in any country where it is not compulsory.

[1] *The Burman.*

It is rare to find a man who cannot read and write. Higher education is backward, though of late substantial advance has been made.

The great majority of Burmans live in villages. A Burmese village normally consists of a single irregular street of houses, thatched buildings of wood, matting, or bamboo, raised from the ground on posts. Except where the houses are widely scattered, every village is surrounded by a fence, generally of split bamboo, sometimes of cactus. At each end of the street is a gate closed at night and supposed to be guarded by a watchman.

The dress of a man consists of a large piece of silk or cotton worn as a skirt. The more voluminous garment is a *paso*, the less ample a *lôngyi*. He wears also a jacket and wound round his head a kerchief called a *gaungbaung*. The women wear skirts called *tamein* and white jackets. They wear no head covering but a flower in the hair is often a pleasing adornment. Burmese males are tattooed on their thighs and frequently on other parts of the body. Often tattoo marks are traced as charms against lethal weapons. Professional thieves frequently have a cat tattooed on each thigh. One cat they pat on entering the house they are about to burgle, the other on emerging with their booty.

Fig. 52. Tattooing.

Burmese women are not tattooed. All Burmans smoke and most chew betel.

For more than a thousand years, the Burmese maintained unaltered the characteristics of their race. Writing of their customs in the 9th century of our era, a Chinese annalist describes them as devout Buddhists, disliking to take animal life; with many monasteries into which all boys go at the age of seven years. The white elephant is pictured with some exaggeration. The dress of men and women is similar to that of the present day. "The women twist their hair high upon the crown of the head, and ornament it with strings of pearls; they wear a natural tinted female petticoat, and throw pieces of delicate silk over themselves; when walking they hold a fan[1]." Ralph Fitch's descriptions of Burmese life in the 16th century might have been written yesterday.

Among the mass of the people, the national type persists. But contact with the west has begun the process of disintegration. Among the educated and semi-educated classes, probably there has been more change in the last ten years than in the preceding ten centuries. Till quite lately, Burmans took no interest in politics and inclined to prefer personal rule. There were periodical petty risings headed by some real or pretended member of the Royal House. But there was no constitutional agitation or desire for representative government. Above all things, the Burman abhorred the suggestion of Indian influence. Of late, national aspirations have become loudly vocal, and clamour for reforms insistent. Burmans have condescended to be inspired by Indian agitators. Leagues and Associations for political propaganda have been formed and the Press has thrown off all restraint. These phenomena must be recorded. It would be premature and unbecoming to comment.

Karens. The next largest section of the population in-

[1] *Burma.* E. H. Parker, 13.

cludes Karens and kindred tribes, numbering rather more than 1,100,000. Their home is Karenni, still occupied by Bghai Karens and wild Padaung and Brè or Laku. The Padaung are remarkable for the practice adopted by the women of wearing from five to five and twenty coils of brass round their necks. Other Karens, Sgau and Pwo, have spread over the plain country of Tenasserim and the Irrawaddy Delta. Formerly a backward, savage race, these

Fig. 53. Padaung house.

classes have come under the civilizing influence of Christian missions and are now loyal, law-abiding, and progressive. They are excellent farmers and, more readily subject to discipline than Burmans, have for many years been trained as military police and, to a less extent, as regular soldiers. "There is an evident tendency for Karen women to be more largely employed in fields than Burmans[1]."

Taungthu. Taungthu, a Karen race, numbering 183,000, originally came from Thatôn in Lower Burma, and are still

[1] *Myaungyma Settlement Report.*

found in that district. But most of them are now in the Myelat, the western borderland of the Southern Shan States, and in the Shan State of Hsa-tung (Thatôn).

Shans. Shans come next with a population of nearly a million. Closely akin to the Siamese, they now mainly occupy the Shan plateau, though traces of their old dominion still exist in Upper Burma, and there are Shan settlements in the plain country. Shans are typically traders rather than agriculturists. Their civilization is somewhat backward but they are making gradual progress. In flapping straw hats and baggy trousers, they pose as picturesque swashbucklers but are not nearly so fierce as they look. They are even more ferociously tattooed than Burmans. An interesting custom in the Shan country, which prevails also further east but not among Burmans, is the holding of a bazaar or market every fifth day. Bazaar day is not unlike market day in an English provincial town, but more brilliant. From far and near in picturesque crowds buyers and sellers flock to the meeting place. One of the most famous of these bazaars is held at Kēngtūng, far to the east across the Salween, where thousands congregate, strange folk from the hills, La and Wa, and people of other uncouth tribes, mingling with the predominant Shan. At Namkham on the border of Bhamo, at Mogôk, and at Maymyo, also, notable bazaars are held.

Intha. A curious tribe in the Shan country is the Intha, lake dwellers, who live in houses built over the Inle lake in Yawnghwe. They are said originally to have come from Tavoy in Lower Burma, brought as captives of war. The custom by which they are best known is that of paddling a boat in a curious way. The paddlers stand in the boat and propel it by their legs twisted round long paddles. A good crew paddling in the usual way will generally outpace an equal number of leg paddlers.

Danu and **Kadu.** Danu and Kadu, tribes of Shan origin, still linger in Upper Burma, but are dying out.

Chins, to the number of 300,000, hold the broken and difficult country bordering on Assam, Manipur and Bengal. A barbarous, drunken, turbulent people, divided into many tribes and clans, their main occupation in former days was raiding villages in the plains. Among the most important tribes are Tashŏn, Yahow, Baungshe, Kanhow and Sôkte. Chins have given more trouble than any other of the border races. Sir George White, who won the Victoria Cross in Afghanistan, declared them to be the hardest enemy to see and fight that he had ever met. Their subjugation, rendered necessary by their predatory habits, was a laborious work. Even in the last few years troops had to suppress a serious rising. During the war, Chins were recruited for the army, and many went to France as members of a Labour Corps. The southern clans, Chinbôn and Chinbôk, on the Pakôkku border, have a curious custom of tattooing the faces of their women with closely set blue lines. This quaint and disfiguring art was not practised by the martial clans in the north. Apparently the feebler southern tribes were subject to raids by the Burmese and women were tattooed to render them less attractive and less liable to be carried away. The custom seems to be dying out. Tame Chins in settled districts, principally Sandoway and Thayetmyo, are quiet friendly people, careful farmers, whose neat and tidy villages compare favourably with the unkempt hamlets of Burmans[1].

Kachins. Far north are Kachins, a race of mountaineers, hardy, brave, and intelligent, whose pressure on the plains was checked only by our occupation. Numbering no more than about 170,000, they inhabit the hill tracts of Bhamo, Myitkyina, Putao, and Katha, and a substantial area in the Northern Shan States. Their stockaded villages are built on the crests of hills, the long, low, thatched houses accommodating several families. Divided into two sections, Chinpaw and Kha-ku, the five main tribes are Marip,

---

[1] A full account of the Chins is given in the Chin *Gazetteer*.

Lahtawng, Lepai, Nkhum, and Maran. Cognate tribes are Sassan, Maru, Lashi, and Yawyin. In former times, villages and village groups were either *kumsa*, under headmen known as *duwa*, or *kumlao*, wherein no local head was recognized and all tribesmen were free and equal. This distinction has been abolished. All villages are now *kumsa*[1].

Under nominal Burmese rule, Kachins combined the practice of rude agriculture with the levy of blackmail on caravans passing between Burma and China and the exaction of tribute from protected villages at the foot of the

Fig. 54. Nungs of the Tarôn Valley.

hills. Now they have to live by their own industry. Order is kept by military police posts which dominate the country and at the same time afford employment to hillmen, compensating the stoppage of lawless customs. For some years, these wild tribes offered stubborn resistance. But after the success of military operations, tact and sympathy and honourable dealing prevailed and the new order was loyally accepted. For more than twenty years Kachins have

[1] For an account of Kachin manners and customs, see the Myitkyina District *Gazetteer*, W. A. Hertz.

served as military police and have done exceedingly well. In the War, they provided recruits for the Indian army, and it is hoped that before long at least one complete Kachin battalion may be raised.

Of a curious and until recently unknown tribe are the Nung or Khanung, neighbours of the Marus and resembling them in appearance but speaking a different language and more scantily clad. They are found only in the Putao district, inhabiting the mountains on both sides of the 'Nmaikha northward from about lat. 27°, and the mountains about the headwaters of the Malikha, north, east and west of the Hkamti Lōng valley. They have the same general characteristics as the other wild tribes of the north-eastern frontier, that is to say, they are dirty, dirtier even than the Maius, treacherous, and worship *nats*. But they differ from other tribes in being extremely shy and timid. They live in solitary huts and do not congregate in villages. Formerly they were oppressed by the Shans of Hkamti Lōng who captured them and kept them as slaves[1].

Talaings. Talaings, whose rise and fall have been recorded, have now dwindled to 320,000. They are not easily distinguishable from Burmans in appearance, dress, and manners. Many prominent persons among the official and educated classes are of Talaing origin. The Talaing language is still spoken; most commonly in parts of the Amherst district. Multitudes of interesting Talaing inscriptions are extant.

Palaungs. Palaungs, timid, peaceable folk, to the number of 144,000, are found principally in the Northern Shan States and in the Katha district.

Many strange tribes dwell in the hills and are seen at the Shan bazaars. Except in an ethnographic survey, it would be fruitless to catalogue their names; and space is wanting for a description of their peculiar manners and customs. But one remarkable tribe may be mentioned,

---

[1] W. A. Hertz.

the **Wa**, who occupy a tract on the north-eastern frontier, stretching for about a hundred miles along the Salween and some fifty miles in breadth. The Wa country is "a series of mountain ranges running north and south and shelving rapidly down to narrow valleys from two to five thousand feet deep. The villages are all on the slopes." Every village is surrounded by a rampart of earth, six to eight feet high and as many thick; round this is cut a deep

Fig. 55. Yang-sek women from the Shan Hills.

ditch. The only entrance is through a long tunnel. Inside the rampart, from 100 to 300 houses raised on piles, are built without order or design. Outside the village is a line of human skulls mounted on posts; for the best known characteristic of the Wa is the practice of head-hunting. Heads are collected as a protection against evil spirits, the idea being that the ghost of the owner of the head will haunt the place and keep off intruders. The Wa never raid outside their own country. To this may be attributed the immunity of their tract from hostile visitation and its continued freedom from administrative control. The Wa go very lightly clad. They are industrious and, except for their head-hunting proclivity, well behaved. Tame Wa, settled

Fig. 56. Tame Wa family.

in the Shan States on the Salween, have perforce abandoned this barbarous practice[1].

The tolerant Burman welcomes strangers. Those from

[1] All that is known of the savage Wa has been recorded by Sir George Scott, from whose description the bald summary in the text has been abstracted. *In the grip of the Wild Wa*, by G. E. Mitton (Lady Scott), contains a popular but quite accurate account of these curious people.

the west, with good-natured contempt he calls *kala* (bar-
barians). Of many settlers, Indians from all parts of the
Peninsula are most numerous, principally from Madras,
Bengal, and Chittagong, but the Pathan and the Sikh also
wander as far afield. **Mahomedans** number 417,290; more
than half in Rangoon and the Akyab district. Of all
Mahomedans, 59,729 are *zerbadi*, that is, of mixed Burmese
and Indian origin. Ten years ago there were 386,679
Hindus, of whom over 100,000 were in Rangoon. Indians
absorb much of the trade of the towns; and Chetti money-
lenders are encroaching on the land. Many Indian labourers
come annually for field work, returning after the harvest
has been gathered.

Chinese. Chinese number 122,834, the population of this
race having doubled in ten years. Probably it has increased
substantially in the last decade. These settlers come from
the coast ports and from Yünnan which borders on Upper
Burma. Chinese are good citizens and mingle freely with
the Burmese.

Europeans. The European population is scanty, amount-
ing only to 12,790, inclusive of the garrison. To these should
be added 11,107 Anglo-Indians.

(II) LANGUAGES

The languages of the Province are classified under the
Tibeto-Chinese; Austro-Asiatic; and Malaya-Polynesian
families. To the first belong the Tibeto-Burman sub-family,
comprising Burmese, spoken by 8,317,842 with local vari-
ants such as Arakanese and Tavoyan; Chin (296,312);
Kachin (170,144); and other dialects of which the Lolo
group (165,548), spoken by some tribes on the north-
eastern frontier is numerically the most important; and
the Siamese-Chinese sub-family including Karen and Shan,
each spoken by about a million people. The Austro-Asiatic
family is represented by Môn-Hkmer languages, of which

the most noticeable are Talaing (179,443) and Palaung (144,139). Of the Malaya-Polynesian family the only dialect of interest is that spoken by Salôn or Mawken[1]; and even of this the classification is doubtful. Malay is spoken by a few thousand immigrants frequenting the coast of Mergui.

The Burmese language is monosyllabic and has three accents, light, medium, and heavy. It has no inflections and the grammar is generally simple. Of Karen and Shan there are many dialects. The Shan language also is monosyllabic and has five or six tones by which the same word acquires as many totally different meanings.

The principal alphabets of Burma, that is Pyu, Talaing, Burmese, and Shan are, directly or indirectly, derived from the old Telugu-Canarese alphabets of South India. The first two, Pyu and Talaing, were derived directly, the former from the Kadamba alphabet of Vanavāsī in North Canara, to the west of South India; the latter from the alphabet of the Pallavas of Kāñcipura in the east of South India....The Burmese and Shan alphabets, though ultimately going back to old Telugu-Canarese have not been derived directly, but indirectly, and both from the Môn or Talaing alphabet[2].

Of the many dialects spoken by hill tribes it would be unprofitable to give a detailed list.

[1] See p. 45.
[2] *Archaeological Survey Report* (1921). C. Duroiselle.

CHAPTER XIV

FIELDS AND GARDENS

Rice. Rice, the ordinary food of all classes, is the chief staple of cultivation. Grown in every district, it absorbs the energies of farmers and peasants in the flat region of

Fig. 57. Irrigation with water scoop.

Lower Burma, converting it into what has been graphically described as "a howling paddy plain." The main crop is sown in nurseries (*pyogin*) at the beginning of the rains; later, the young shoots are taken up and carefully planted, one by one, at suitable intervals, in the sodden fields which have been ploughed with the aid of buffaloes and bullocks. But often rice is sown broadcast. Each field is separated from its neighbours by a low mound (*kazin*). Harvest comes at the beginning of the cold weather. Of many varieties of rice, *kauk-kyi*, which supplies practically all the crop for export is the most important. In Upper Burma, besides rice grown on fields watered by rainfall, great quantities are raised on irrigated land. In dry districts, a winter crop, *mayin*, is sown in the cold season on the edges of meres and on marshy depressions and reaped in the early rains. In the hills is practised a wasteful form of cultivation known as *taungya*. The trees and undergrowth are cut down and burnt in the dry weather and rice seed is dibbled in as soon as the rains begin. After garnering the crop, the *taungya* cutter usually abandons the field and starts afresh next year on another plot. The same ground is seldom cultivated two years in succession and is not re-visited till at least the undergrowth has sprung up again. It will be understood that this practice may involve the destruction of much valuable forest[1].

The area under rice cultivation is over 10,000,000 acres, of which over 8,000,000 acres are in Lower Burma. The principal rice-growing districts in Lower Burma are Pegu (868,987)[2]; Hanthawaddy (789,385); Myaung-mya (701,563); Bassein (697,572); Pyapôn (660,948); Akyab (656,203); Thatôn (623,803); Insein (530,759); Tharrawaddy (529,224); Henzada (527,361); Amherst (424,491); Toungoo (400,731); Ma-u-bin (392,336); Prome (324,577). In Upper Burma, Shwebo (444,975) with a vast area under irrigation, alone rivals these great rice-producing districts. Katha (183,771) and Yamèthin (176,686) come next but far behind.

The out-turn of rice is enormous and has been increasing almost year by year. The estimated crop in 1921–22 amounted to 6,900,000 tons of paddy. Of this quantity, it was expected that 4,000,000 tons of paddy, or 2,600,000 tons of cargo rice would be available for export.

Dry crops. Though rice is so vastly the most important,

---

[1] But recently successful efforts have been made to utilize *taungya* cultivation for concentrated regeneration of forests.

[2] Figures in brackets show the area in acres under rice in 1920–21.

many other products are cultivated in fields, gardens, and *taungya*. Wheat has long been cultivated in Upper Burma, but not so far back as the 9th century. San Germano remarks that "the wheat of the Kingdom of Ava is most excellent[1]." Crawfurd "found that wheat was cultivated in the vicinity of Ava in considerable quantity....We compared the grain with the Patna wheat which we had along with us, and it was greatly superior both in size and colour[2]." Wheat is grown also in the Shan States with success. It is perhaps surprising that a form of cultivation so long established has not been more largely practised. Other cereals, maize, gram, and millet, red and white, are grown in dry districts. Millet suffers much from the ravages of a small parasite plant called pwinbyu. Many varieties of peas and beans are produced in all parts of the province. The *dani* palm is cultivated in the Irrawaddy Delta.

Sesamum, grown on about 1,000,000 acres is a very valuable crop. About 300,000 acres, principally in Pakôkku, Magwe, and Myingyan, are devoted to ground-nuts of which the out-turn reaches some 100,000 tons. The extension of this cultivation is comparatively recent.

Tea is the staple product of the Shan State of Tawnpeng where it is grown to the annual value of about £200,000, for the purpose of being made into *letpet*, pickled tea, a condiment of universal consumption. Many Europeans profess to find the *durian* delicious and even *ngapi* has its admireis. It is not on record that any one other than a native of Burma has found *letpet* palatable. In Burmese times, *letpet* was brought down by strings of bullocks to the mart at Mandalay. The railway has now superseded this primitive mode of transport. Tea for the European market is not yet produced. Coffee has been grown by Europeans at Toungoo and Bhamo but with only moderate success. Its cultivation in the Northern Shan sub-State of Hsumhsai is very promising.

[1] *The Burmese Empire*, 190.　　　　[2] Crawfurd, 101–2.

Potatoes are cultivated in the Southern Shan States and elsewhere, for instance in Putao. Sugar cane culture is widely distributed.

In most parts of Burma, tobacco is grown on in all about 120,000 acres. The indigenous varieties are of no great value commercially, perhaps because the processes of curing are either imperfectly understood or unskilfully practised. Burmese cheroots are well known, but for the most part are made of imported tobacco. Experiments with Virginia and Havana seed have been only moderately successful. But some of the best Burmese cigars are now made of tobacco grown at Danubyu from this seed and cured

Fig. 58. Burmese cheroot.

locally. Very little tobacco is put into the large green and white cheroots, wrapped in *thanat* leaves, which are smoked by every Burmese man and woman and by many children. No doubt there is a great future for tobacco cultivation in Burma; but it may be remote.

The betel-palm (*Areca catechu*), called by the Burmese *kun*, is widely cultivated and also grows by nature. From association of name and use may here be mentioned the betel vine (*Piper betle*) grown in dry districts and producing betel leaves for chewing. This is a very valuable product.

Cotton is grown largely in Sagaing, Myingyan, Meiktila, Lower Chindwin, and Thayetmyo, to a less extent elsewhere. The area under cotton is about 300,000 acres, the annual out-turn about 12,000 tons.

Rubber is grown with success in plantations in Mergui,

Hanthawaddy, Amherst, Toungoo, and elsewhere. The first experiments were made in Government plantations in Arakan, Mergui and Rangoon. The Mergui plantation has been acquired by a Company.

Fruits. Fruits abound in rich and varied profusion. Most widely distributed is the plantain (banana) which is cultivated everywhere. Plantains vary in quality; some kinds are of excellent flavour; others are hardly fit to offer to a pony. A somewhat similar judgement may be passed on the mango, except that it is not offered to ponies. The ordinary mango with a flavour of turpentine is worthless. The best kind is one of the most delicious fruits. From the extreme south come the durian (*Durio Zibethinus*) and the mangosteen (*Garcinia mangostana*). So highly esteemed by Burmans is the *durian* that, in the king's time, as soon as the fruit ripened, a steamer was chartered every year to bring a cargo of the dainty for the Court at Mandalay. As already mentioned, some Europeans profess a morbid passion for this fruit. To others, its scent and taste alike are inexpressibly loathsome. The mangosteen, by universal consent, is the most delicate and exquisite of eastern fruits. Coco-nuts abound; pine-apples, custard-apples (*Anona squamosa*), pleasant but somewhat insipid, marian, jack fruit, papaya (*Carica papaya*) of peptic virtue, guavas, and pomegranates are plentiful. Allied to the custard-apple, the *chirimoya* of Peru (*Anona cherimolia*) has been introduced and is cultivated but not to any great extent. Oranges grow best in the Northern Shan States; less successfully elsewhere, as in the Southern Shan States, Chin Hills, and Amherst. Limes and citrons are cultivated in the hills. Mulberries are grown by Yabein[1] in Magwe and Thayetmyo; but for the sake of the leaves to feed silk-worms, not for the fruit. The bael tree, of

---

[1] *Yabein* are of Burmese stock, dwellers on the western slopes of the Pegu Yoma; despised on account of their practice of destroying silk-worms in the course of their silk culture.

which the fruit is valued for medicinal properties, is also cultivated.

Of vegetables and miscellaneous products may be specified chillies, onions, capsicum, mustard, sweet potatoes (*Ipomoea batatas*), yams (*Dioscorea*), brinjals (*Solanum Melongena*), tomatoes, turmeric, ginger, cinnamon, cucumbers, melons, pumpkins.

Poppies grow luxuriantly in the Shan States and Kachin Hills, where opium is consumed apparently without ill-effects. The cultivation of the poppy in the Kachin Hills has recently been declared illegal.

Department of Agriculture. The interests of agriculture are committed to the charge of a special Department under a Director and controlled by the Development Commissioner. Among the aims of the Department are, the amelioration of agricultural conditions, the encouragement of experiments with new products, the introduction of modern scientific implements, the improvement of indigenous staples. The Department is about to be strengthened and reorganized. When thoroughly equipped, it will include 17 Imperial, 19 Provincial, and 188 subordinate officers. In a country where the bulk of the population depends for subsistence on fields, gardens, and orchards, the scope for the energies of the Department is unlimited.

CHAPTER XV

OCCUPATIONS OF THE PEOPLE

THE great majority of the people of Burma are farmers and peasants, dwellers in villages. Out of a total population of about 12,000,000 as enumerated in 1911, only rather more than a million were townsmen. The remainder constituted the rural population of whom about 8,500,000 were returned as occupied with pasture and agriculture or dependent thereon. The main occupation, agriculture, is the subject of the last chapter. Here we deal with other arts and crafts.

Dependent on the supply of rice is the important rice-milling industry which flourishes at Rangoon and the other principal ports. This is not an indigenous occupation, being directed almost exclusively by European firms; but it gives employment to large numbers of workers, Burmans, and immigrants. Other industries which owe their prosperity to foreign influences are oil-winning and oil-refining; cotton-ginning; and the conversion of timber at saw-mills. The extent to which mining is pursued has been indicated in the chapter on Minerals. Similarly, the extraction of timber for local use and export, and cutch boiling, in both of which many Burmans are employed, have been mentioned in the pages devoted to forests.

Next to agriculture fishing is the greatest native industry. It is carried on mainly in the Delta of the Irrawaddy and on the sea coast. Dependent on this is the manufacture of *ngapi* or fish paste.

Of indigenous handicrafts, boat-building, cart-making and the fashioning of rude ploughs and other agricultural implements, are widely spread. The making of *byit* (fringes) of *dani* leaves for walls and roofs of houses is practised where *dani* is cultivated. There are, it is hardly necessary to say, Burmese carpenters and blacksmiths. But the best carpenters are Chinese. The Burman puts up his own house of bamboo, timber, mat and thatch; and Burmese masons build pagodas and other sacred edifices.

Weaving etc. The home industries of cotton- and silk-weaving were formerly universal. Every house had its loom whereon the girls wove *pasos* and *tameins*, the skirts worn by men and women respectively, and produced textures of bright and beautiful colours. Some of the elaborate silken webs are of exquisite design. It is to be regretted that these have to a great extent been supplanted by imported fabrics often of inferior kinds. Of late, there has been a revival of this occupation. There is a small school of silk-weaving at Amarapura; and silk weaving is now practised with profit. Co-operative credit societies of weavers have been formed and "the industry is regaining lost ground[1]." Gay and graceful umbrellas are made. For a time these were almost entirely displaced by common ugly European articles. But this industry, also, is reviving[2]. Kalaga (curtains) are made of cloth; some of the *appliqué* work on them is of a high standard. Bags of beautiful design, ornamented with bead patterns, are produced in the Shan country. In the Chin and Kachin Hills are woven *saung*, rough sheets, useful and of interesting patterns.

Cheroot making is a home industry widely practised. Basket- and mat-weaving are important occupations yielding pleasing and useful products. The delicate *thin-byu* mats made at Danubyu on the Irrawaddy have long been famous. More than a hundred years ago Symes wrote: "Donabew...is...celebrated for its manufactory of mats, which are made here in beautiful variety, and superior in

---

[1] *Burmese village industries.* Paper read by Mr A. P. Morris before the Royal Society of Arts, January 2nd, 1920.

[2] *Ibid.*

Fig. 59. Weaving.

quality to what are fabricated in any other part of the [Burmese] Empire[1]."

Pottery. Pottery attains the dignity of an art and besides pans and jars of common use produces many articles of ornate or grotesque design. Of the large Pegu jars, Symes writes: "The jars of Pegu are in general estimation throughout India, being remarkable for their size and excellence[2]." "The bulk of the glazed pottery work is done by Talaings or in areas where the work has been started by Talaings. Kyaukmyaung, the most important centre in Upper Burma, was settled by Talaing captives[3]." Bassein and Twante used to be important centres of the pottery industry but have declined. "Most of the Burma clays are coloured, yellow predominating; the chief colouring being iron. When burned they give varying shades of red from a bright brick red to an orange tint[4]." But black and green ware also is made. Some articles are beaten into shape; others are turned on the potter's wheel. The glazing material used is either galena or lead slag. The industry is of ancient date, specimens having survived for over four hundred years.

Workers in brass and iron are engaged in making bells and gongs, images of the Buddha, and *das* (knives) of all shapes and sizes. Burmese bells are notable for beauty of tone and for graceful shape. The making of bronze statuettes is a comparatively modern industry[5].

Silver-work. Even more than for crafts whose end is utility, Burmans are renowned for art-work. Without, perhaps, rivalling the idealism of China or Japan, Burmese artists, subject to their limitations, attain a high standard of excellence. Two of the most widely-practised and effective arts are silver-work and wood-carving. At the capitals,

---

[1] Symes, 452.   [2] Symes, 91 n.
[3] A. P. Morris. *Journal of the Burma Research Society*, VIII. (III.), 1918).
[4] *Ibid.*
[5] A. P. Morris. *Burmese village industries, ut sup.*

as might be expected, are assembled most of the silver
workers but many a smaller town has artists of local repute.
Bowls, betel and lime boxes, ornamented with figures of
men and animals, flowers, foliage, and scroll work of bold
yet delicate design, in high relief, are typical specimens of
Burmese silver ware. There is a risk that this rare and
beautiful art may be debased by western teaching and by

Fig. 60. Wood-carving.

misguided efforts at encouragement and improvement.
Silver tea-pots and cigar cases, with Burmese ornamentation, can give no joy to cultured taste. Charming *niello*
work is done, chiefly at Prome. Gold work is less common;
but ear-tubes, ear-rings, bracelets and necklaces, golden
chains of honour (*shwe salwè*) are made by native artists.
Sometimes the gold of ornaments is dyed red with tamarind
juice.

Wood-carving. As famous and as beautiful as silver-work

is the elaborate wood-carving of intricate pattern which adorns monasteries and public buildings. Some of the most beautiful examples are at the Queen's Monastery at Mandalay; but the finest are said to be at the Salin Monastery in that town. Carved wooden figures, often grotesque, of *bilu* (demons) and *nats*, are also characteristic; and boxes adorned with carvings are common. Ivory-carving of great

Fig. 61. A corner of the palace, Mandalay.

delicacy and of exquisite finish, is produced, mostly at Rangoon and Moulmein.

Lacquer-work. Lovely lacquer ware is made at Pagan, the most famous centre, as well as in the Lower Chindwin, at Laikha in the Southern Shan States, and elsewhere. Lacquer workers are about 7000 in number; of whom some 1500 are at Pagan. Bowls, trays, betel-boxes, tables, and boxes for storing manuscripts, covered with rich pictures

and designs, are among the many lacquered articles produced. For bowls, the framework is of very fine woven
bamboo, mingled in the best specimens with horse-hair.
On this are imposed successive layers of the exudation of
the *thitsi* tree. On the lacquer surface a pattern is worked
by successive incisions filled with colouring matter, orange,
yellow, red, black, or green. The process is painfully slow

Fig. 62. Carving Buddhas.

and laborious; the effect is admirable. The industry is said
to have been brought to Pagan in the middle of the 11th
century. A tube of lacquer work dated 1274 A.D. has been
found there in a pagoda[1].

Images of the Buddha, of conventional types, are carved

[1] For an elaborate account of Burmese lacquer work see a paper
by Mr A. P. Morris, *Journal of the Burma Research Society*, IX. i.
(1919).

at Amarapura and elsewhere. The materials used are marble and steatite.

In pictorial art, so far, Burmans have not attained a high standard. But there are native frescoes and pictures more quaint and grotesque than beautiful. Some frescoes on the walls and ceilings of *zayats* (rest houses) near the Shwe Dagôn Pagoda, representing the torments of lost souls, are realistically horrible. And there are many old frescoes at Pagan. One thing a Burmese artist can do. He can draw an elephant. An art school has been opened at Rangoon. It is possible that Burmese pictorial art has a future.

CHAPTER XVI

(I) TRADE AND COMMERCE[1]

(The figures in this section are generally approximate. Except when otherwise stated they refer to the year 1920–21, called also "last year.")

WITH a people enjoying a comparatively high standard of living and demanding many varied articles of subsistence, luxury, comfort, and display; with a fertile country yielding in great quantities products sought by other nations; aided and stimulated by European and Indian capital and enterprise, Burma ranks as a commercial country of some importance. Its trade is of modern growth, sprung into luxuriance from small beginnings, since the British occupation of Pegu (1852).

Sea-borne trade. Rangoon, admirably situated as the collecting depot for provincial produce and as the distributing centre for imports, absorbs the greatest part of the sea-borne trade with India and with British and foreign ports, its share approximating to nine-tenths of the total. Of the minor ports, Bassein, Akyab, and Moulmein, each claims from 2 to 3 per cent. of the foreign[2] and from 4 to 6 per cent. of the Indian trade. Mergui and Tavoy have a small foreign and Indian trade, but with Sandoway and Kyaukpyu they take a moderate share of inter-provincial coasting trade, Mergui's portion approaching one-fifth of the whole. Victoria Point, the remote port of Tenasserim, has a small import traffic, almost exclusively with the Straits Settlements; and a little export trade with the United Kingdom, the Straits Settlements, and Siam. Last year the value of the sea-borne trade with foreign and Indian

[1] See Appendix V.

[2] Except where otherwise stated, "foreign" includes all trade except Indian and inter-provincial.

ports reached the respectable total of over £100,000,000, the highest recorded in the history of the Province.

Imports. Although Burma produces all that is necessary to support life in health and to maintain a reasonably high standard of comfort, goods to the value of over £44,000,000 were imported. Most freely sent by foreign countries and India are cotton, twist and yarn, and manufactured; into Rangoon alone these imports were valued at over £7,500,000 (foreign) and over £5,250,000 (Indian). Imported piece goods from Europe and Japan compete successfully with local manufactures. Silk to the value of over £800,000 came chiefly, in the raw state, from China, manufactured, from Japan. The revival of silk-weaving increases the demand for raw silk which the local production is insufficient to supply. Woollen goods, mostly manufactured, came to the value of over £600,000; about four-fifths from the United Kingdom, Japan and Holland being the next large contributors. India sent jute manufactures to the value of nearly £2,000,000.

Liquors have always been poured in profusely; probably their use among the native population is increasing. In the year before the War, over 1,600,000 gallons were imported; then naturally the quantity declined; but there has been a gradual revival; and last year 760,463 gallons of all kinds of alcoholic liquors, mostly ale, beer, and porter, valued at nearly £600,000 came to Rangoon.

Metals, principally iron and steel, but including also zinc, brass, copper, tin and lead, were imported to the value of over £4,000,000; while machinery, mill work and hardware came in to the value of over £3,000,000. Motor cars have become very popular; over 1200, valued at above £830,000, were imported. America sends most of these, but cars of English make come in rising numbers.

Other imports include salt, grain and pulse, coal, tobacco, mineral oils, earthenware, glass, matches, soap, and umbrellas. But it will be understood that many other miscellaneous goods appear in the trade returns.

Exports. Burma has valuable products to exchange for imports and finds markets in all quarters of the globe. Last year the value of the private export trade amounted to nearly £53,000,000, showing a substantial balance in favour of the province. **Rice** is scattered over the world in lavish profusion. Besides all parts of the British Empire, more than twenty foreign countries compete in this trade. In a good year the quantity exported rises to 2½ millions of tons. Last year it was somewhat less, but the value amounted to £31,679,200. In years of scarcity, India takes a large proportion, sometimes more than half of the total. Ceylon, the Straits Settlements, and the United Kingdom are the largest foreign buyers.

Next in order, but at a long interval, are **mineral oils** and associated products. Of mineral oils, some 160 million gallons; of paraffin wax some 25,000 tons; of candles some five million pounds, are exported yearly to the aggregate value of about £7,250,000. There are, it need hardly be said, fluctuations. Last year the quantity of oils and wax exported was less than usual, while there was a decrease which may be permanent in the export of candles. By far the largest quantity of mineral oils is absorbed by India; practically all the kerosine and nearly half the benzine and petrol.

Teak has long been a staple export. Last year the quantity sent out of the Province amounted to 227,297 cubic tons valued at over £3,750,000. In other years, the quantity has barely exceeded 100,000 tons. Large exports to India to some extent accounted for the high figures of last year.

When the potential mineral resources of the country are remembered, the trade in metals is disappointing. The export of tin does not greatly exceed in value £100,000; wolfram was exported during the War to the value of over £1,000,000 a year, but hardly more than £12,000 worth was sent out in 1921–22. Last year the export of lead rose to nearly 25,000 tons valued at about £1,000,000 and 3000 tons of zinc, valued at £22,600, were sent to Belgium. All the jadeite, nearly 4500 cwt., valued at £164,000, goes to China.

During the War and for a year or two after there was a brisk trade in hides and skins. But of late there has been a serious decline. In 1920–21, the value was only about £250,000 as compared with over £1,000,000 in the preceding year. There was a further decline in 1921–22.

From 7000 to 14,000 tons of raw cotton are exported yearly, the quantity varying with the harvest. Last year only 9000 tons, valued at £1,125,000, were exported from Rangoon. Most of the cotton goes to the United Kingdom but Japan is an intermittent purchaser, taking 33 tons in 1916–17, 6461 tons in 1919–20, and 2889 tons in 1920–21. China took 1200 tons by sea and rather more overland.

Of agricultural products other than rice, ground nuts and their subsidiaries are important, though the export trade is not nearly so good as before the War. Last year, of the estimated crop of 117,630 tons, hardly 5000 tons were exported, mostly to the United Kingdom. Of ground-nut oil the exports vary in a surprising way from year to year. For example, Rangoon exported to foreign ports in 1919–20 over 600,000 gallons valued at £230,000; last year, less than 50,000 gallons worth about £17,000. Similarly the quantity and value of ground-nut oil-cake (30,000 tons and £300,000) were far less than in previous years. In beans, there is still, in spite of a recent fall, a large trade, much more flourishing than before the War. In 1919–20, over 100,000 tons, valued at nearly £2,000,000, were sent to foreign countries. Last year, the quantity was only about 33,000 tons and the value not much over £400,000. But India also takes substantial quantities.

Among other miscellaneous articles of export may be mentioned rubber (about 1800 tons.); cutch; and lac.

The British Empire still contributes the bulk of the imports, over 60 per cent. The latest figures indicate that this superiority may be maintained or even increased. Last year from the United Kingdom alone imports to the value of £16,250,000 came to Rangoon; from the Empire, £18,000,000. The United States contributed £3,500,000 worth. European countries sent goods to the value of nearly £3,000,000; Holland coming first with nearly £1,000,000; followed by Germany with £600,000; and Belgium with £323,000. Asian imports were valued at £3,300,000, of which Japan contributed more than £2,600,000.

The British Empire is also by far the best customer, and appears to be regaining ground lost temporarily during the War, absorbing last year 80 per cent. of the export trade of Rangoon. The United Kingdom, Ceylon, and the Straits Settlements take the largest proportion. The share of other European countries is only about 10 per cent. of the total; Germany coming first with £750,000 from Rangoon alone; Belgium and Italy following with about £300,000. Japan is a fairly constant customer to the extent of over £1,000,000. With the United States the export trade fluctuates in a rather remarkable way. Averaging £372,700 in three previous years, rising to £542,100 in 1919–20, the value fell to £109,800 last year.

With India, the total trade in recent years has varied from £21,000,000 to £42,000,000; Bengal, Bombay and Madras, in that order dividing almost the whole.

It may be interesting to give a paragraph to German trade. Before the War many German firms were established in Rangoon and the other ports, competing on equal terms and successfully with British merchants. Naturally, these firms disappeared at the outbreak of war. The latest returns show, however, that Germany has begun again to trade with Burma. Last year, from that country came shipments of hardware (£73,000), machinery and mill-work (over £100,000), salt (over £100,000), beer (58,000 gallons), woollen goods (over £20,000). Germany was by far the largest foreign (as distinct from British) buyer of rice, taking 50,000 tons, valued at £780,000. Besides a small quantity of rice bran and teak, she also took nearly 10,000 tons of beans. In imports to Burma from Europe (exclusive of the United Kingdom), as already noted, Germany was second only to Holland and in exports was easily first. But only two German vessels came to Rangoon last year.

Overland trade. Overland trade is carried on with western China and Siam, in about equal proportions. The volume of trade is comparatively small, approaching in value £2,000,000 a year each way. Trade is registered at frontier stations. As there is no railway communication, caravans of mules and pack bullocks are the principal means of transport. The only imports of interest are raw silk from China and elephants from Siam. Except jadeite of which about 600 cwt. goes to China, exports are somewhat dull, raw cotton, twist, and yarn, and piece goods being the only articles of any note.

For statistical purposes, trade with unadministered Kachin country, the Shan States, and Karenni is registered at many stations. The imports of interest are lead from the Bawdwin mines, *letpet* (pickled tea), potatoes, *thanatpet* (for cigar wrappers) and oranges. From Karenni comes a fair quantity of wolfram. Piece goods are practically the only articles sent in exchange.

(II) LIGHTHOUSES

The coast of Burma is sufficiently well lighted. The entrance to the harbour of Akyab is marked by a lighthouse on Savage Island. Fifteen miles away is Oyster Island. South of Cape Negrais are Alguada and China Bakir, at the mouth of the China Bakir or To River. Eastern Grove marks the east entrance of the Rangoon River. In the Bay of Bengal, two miles from the Cocos, is

Table Island. Off the Amherst coast are Double Island, twelve miles south of Amherst and seven miles from land; and Green Island, near Amherst Point. At the entrance of the Tavoy river is the light on Reef Island.

The oldest lighthouse is Savage Island, built in 1842; the newest Green Island in 1903. The first lighthouse on Oyster Reef was destroyed by a cyclone in 1884.

There are also lightships off the Baragua Flats and Krishna Shoal, south of the mouths of the Irrawaddy; and at the entrance to the Rangoon River.

CHAPTER XVII

CANALS AND EMBANKMENTS

(I) CANALS

Navigation. FOR navigation, the only important artificial waterway is the **Twante** canal, which runs for 22
miles from the Rangoon River by way of the Kanaungto
creek to the Irrawaddy at Twante. When first constructed
it was practicable only by boats and shallow-draught
launches with which, in the busy season, it was over-
crowded. Recently it has been deepened and widened; now
its breadth is 300 feet, except at the chord cut from the
Kanaungto creek to the Rangoon river which has a breadth
of only 180 feet; and its depth is 6 feet below the level of
ordinary Spring tides. Except the largest steamers all river
craft adopt this alternative route instead of the Bassein
creek[1]. Tolls are levied on all vessels using this canal. In
1920–21, the gross revenue amounted to £53,350.

In the Pegu district, the Pegu-Sittaing canal connects
the Pegu and Sittaing rivers. A small canal in Thatôn,
from the Sittang to the town of Kyaikto, as already noted,
has been ruined by the bore of the Sittang. In Mandalay
the Obo canal may also be mentioned.

Irrigation. From time immemorial, the dry tracts of
Upper Burma have been watered by irrigation systems
planned by native engineers, often with considerable in-
genuity. Under the slack rule of Burmese kings many of
these decayed or deteriorated. Very soon after the annexation, the attention of highly skilled officers of the
Indian Irrigation Department was devoted to the improvement of native systems and the initiation of fresh projects
on scientific lines. The **Mandalay** canal was first completed.

---

[1] See p. 27.

Fig. 63. The Obo canal.

Thirty-nine miles in length, constructed at the cost of £570,000 and finished in the year 1902, it waters an area of 62,000 acres and returns annually 6 per cent. on the capital outlay.

The **Shwebo** canal, which draws its supplies from the Mu river, has converted 170,000 acres of Shwebo from dry desert to fertile rice fields. It cost £600,000, and its annual return is 8·3 per cent. The **Ye-u** canal is under construction on the right bank of the Mu and was partly opened in 1918–19. It will irrigate 109,000 acres at the cost of £572,300.

In Minbu the **Môn**, **Man**, and **Salin** canals have been completed, with much difficulty, at the cost of £566,800, and have brought under cultivation some 60,000 acres. Most, if not all, of these projects are based on old native works, vastly improved.

The total area irrigated from major canals in 1920–21 was 329,000 acres producing crops estimated in value at £1,275,000.

Many minor irrigation works have been adapted from Burmese originals. Of these, the most important is the network of canals in Kyauksè by which almost the whole district is watered. It has not been found practicable to utilize the Irrawaddy or the Chindwin for irrigation on a large scale.

Formerly the dry districts of Upper Burma were subject to recurring seasons of scarcity. In Shwebo, for instance, in about one year in three, the rains failed and the able-bodied population migrated for field work to the rich plains of Lower Burma, sending due part of their earnings for the support of their families left behind. But the Burman clings to his home and back went the migrants after harvest, hoping for a better season next year. Now, in most of the arid tracts, irrigation, extension of dry cultivation, and improved communications have dispelled fear of famine.

(II) Embankments

Embankments. On the right bank of the Irrawaddy a series of embankments has been constructed for the protection of culturable land from floods caused by the rise of the river in the rains. Starting from Kyangin, the embankments run past Myanaung and Henzada to the mouth of the Pantanaw creek in Ma-u-bin for 122 miles. Other embankments, nearly 80 and 40 miles respectively in length protect Ma-u-bin and Thôngwa Islands. On Ma-u-bin Island alone the protected area is over 120,000 acres. Along the Nagwun (Bassein) river runs yet another embankment for 76 miles. These works bring under cultivation a large expanse of rich rice land to the estimated extent of over 800,000 acres yielding a great return to the people in crops and to Government in revenue. The value of the rice crop on the reclaimed area was estimated in 1920–21 at £3,300,000. Yandoon Island is to be protected by an embankment estimated to cost £103,870, to reclaim 70,000 acres, and to yield a return of 12 per cent.

After long discussion, it was decided many years ago not to embank the left bank of the Irrawaddy, the effect of confining on both sides so large a river being feared. Lately this question has been re-opened and a project for protecting the left bank has been sanctioned. This work is expected to cost £620,000, to safeguard 500,000 acres, and to yield 20 per cent. on the outlay. A similar scheme, the Gyaing-Ataran-Salween embankment and reclamation, near Moulmein, is under consideration.

CHAPTER XVIII

RAILWAYS AND ROADS

Railways. PARTLY because of its unrivalled waterways, partly because in the dry season the ordinary Burmese springless bullock cart, often on solid wheels, can be driven over the reaped fields, mostly because for many years Burma was hardly treated by the Imperial Government and allowed a share of its revenues too scant to provide adequately for its development, the Province is still insufficiently equipped in the matter of land communication. It was not till 1877, more than fifty years after the acquisition of Tenasserim and Arakan, a quarter of a century after the conquest of Pegu, that the first **railway** from Rangoon to Prome, 161 miles in length, was opened. In the next seven or eight years a line was built from Rangoon to Pegu and extended to Toungoo which, at a distance of about 160 miles, had up to that time been more than a week's journey from the capital. Owing entirely to the insistence of Sir Charles Bernard, the continuation of this line to Mandalay was taken in hand in the first year of the occupation of Upper Burma. The country being flat and engineering difficulties few, the whole length to Mandalay (384 miles) was completed and opened for traffic early in 1889. From Mandalay a line runs through Maymyo to Lashio, the headquarters of the Northern Shan States (180 miles). From the foot of the hills to the Maymyo plateau the line zigzags up the side of the cliffs, with the inevitable corkscrew. The intention was to continue the line as far as the Salween at Kunlôn Ferry, with the design of piercing China and reaching Talifu. But doubts were cast on the commercial possibilities of the project, and the line remains suspended in mid-air at Lashio.. One of its most striking features is the famous viaduct at Gôk-teik. In length 1620 feet, this stands 325 feet over a natural bridge of rock, itself some 500 feet above the bottom of the gorge which it spans. Far below are a torrent and caves hung with stalactites. From the railway are seen the lovely waterfalls of the Myitngè. A branch runs to the lead mines at Bawdwin.

Fig. 64. A Railway Station.

From Mandalay a short line runs to Amarapura, linked by a steam ferry with Sagaing whence starts the railway to Myitkyina in the far north, 724 miles from Rangoon. This line passes through Shwebo, the old land-locked Shan State of Wuntho, and Mogaung, the jadeite depot, sending a branch from Naba to the river at Katha. A daily ferry service connects Katha with Bhamo. Branch lines run from Thazi on the Mandalay railway, through Meiktila to

Myingyan on the Irrawaddy; from Sagaing to Alôn on the Chindwin; from Pegu through Thatôn to Martaban, opposite Moulmein. A line connects Bassein with Henzada and Kyangin on the Irrawaddy; and Henzada connects

Fig. 65. On the Southern Shan States Railway.

with a branch of the Prome line by a railway ferry. So one can travel by rail from Rangoon to Bassein, Bhamo, and Myitkyina, but in each case with the aid of a ferry service. Some day the long projected bridge over the Irrawaddy at Sagaing will be accomplished and unbroken railway communication between Rangoon and Myitkyina will be established.

From Thazi, already mentioned, starts a line to the Southern Shan States. It has been completed only as far as Heho in the State of Yawnghwe, part of the work having been done by Turkish prisoners of war. An extension towards the Yawnghwe valley is being surveyed.

The total length of railways, all on the metre gauge, is 1605 miles, quite inadequate for so large a country. Arakan has one very small line, a few miles in length; Mergui and Tavoy have no railways. Lines from Pyinmana to Taungdwingyi; from Alon to Saingbyin in the direction of Yeu; from Moulmein to Ye in Tavoy, are to be built immediately out of profits made by Government from rice control during the War.

Projects for linking Burma with China, with India, and with Siam have long been under discussion. In process of time, a railway will no doubt be built from Chittagong through the Arakan Division to, or near to, Akyab, and thence to the Irrawaddy opposite Prome, where the river may be bridged. With China, but perhaps not for many years, railway communication, when established, will connect Bhamo with Tengyüeh, Talifu, and Yünnanfu. The difficulties of this route have been ascertained not to be insuperable.

The lines to Prome and to Mandalay have yielded handsome returns from the outset. Burmans take kindly to railway travelling and on an average the whole population travels by rail twice a year. Except in the neighbourhood of Rangoon, trains do not run very frequently. In some places, there is only one train a day in each direction; in others, there are not more than two or three trains a week. The easy-going Burman sits contentedly on the platform for half the day awaiting the arrival of the fire-carriage (*mi-yata*).

Roads. The total length of metalled roads is 1972 miles.

Of unmetalled roads, 10,570 miles are reckoned. Many of these are merely rough tracks, clouded with dust in the dry weather, soaked with mud in the rains. The principal metalled roads are those from Rangoon to Prome; from

Fig. 66. On the road to Fort Hertz.

Rangoon to Pegu; from Mandalay to Maymyo; from Thazi to Taung-gyi; from Thabeik-kyin to Mogôk. The three roads last mentioned wind along hill sides, between lofty cliffs and sheer precipices, with many curves. They are quite practicable for motor traffic. The road from Myitkyina to Fort Hertz (Putao) is a mule-track.

CHAPTER XIX

CHIEF TOWNS

Lower Burma

Rangoon. RANGOON is still the capital of Burma and the headquarters of the Local Government. Although it is only since the British conquest of Pegu that the city has risen to great importance, it was long a place of some note[1]. The dawn of its history is in the year 585 B.C., when the first Shwe Dagôn Pagoda was built, and round it sprang up a village or small town. It was not till 1755 A.D. that it acquired its present name. In that year Alaungpaya laid out a new town on the river bank and called it *Yan-gôn*, the end of strife. Not long after, the East India Company established a factory and 1796 saw the appointment of a British Resident or Agent. At the time of Captain Symes' visit in 1794, Rangoon was a busy trading port, with some twenty-five to thirty thousand inhabitants, extending for about a mile along the river and about a third of a mile in depth. Inland, the square city (*myo*), characteristic of Burmese royal towns, was enclosed by a wooden stockade. The houses were raised from the ground on posts, some of bamboo, some of wood. Pigs roamed the streets and acted as scavengers. The description is strangely familiar to those who saw Mandalay in 1885. Later on, the town languished, probably on account of Burmese misrule, and in 1826 its population had dwindled to about 8000. It was a miserable place in a dismal swamp. After the First Burmese War, it began to revive. In 1841, King Tharrawaddy built a new stockaded city near the great Pagoda, and part of the

[1] For an admirable and interesting account of "Old Rangoon," by Prof. W. G. Fraser, see *Journal of the Burma Research Society*, x. ii.

town was transferred to the new site. By the time of the Second War (1852), the town was about as populous as in 1794. After the annexation of Pegu, it was laid out by Colonel Fraser on a definite and well-conceived plan allowing for further expansion.

The present city stands on the Rangoon River, twenty-one miles from the sea. It is the fourth town in India, in point of population. In the last thirty or forty years, it has entirely changed its character. In 1881 the population was 134,176, the larger proportion consisting of Buddhists. In 1911 the inhabitants numbered 293,316, of whom 108,350 were Hindus, 97,467 Buddhists, and 54,634 Mahomedans. In 1921 the population had increased to 341,962. Rangoon is now a cosmopolitan city, full of men of strange races and many tongues. The business part of the town lies along the north side of the river, stretching from Kemmendine and Alôn on the west to Pazundaung on the east. Here are great rice mills, timber and oil depots, warehouses of imported goods, wharves and jetties, banks, shops, printing presses, offices. On the opposite bank is the busy industrial suburb of Dalla, a place of note before Rangoon was founded. The prosperity of Rangoon is mainly due to British, and, to a minor extent, Indian, commercial enterprise. The Burmese have had no part in it. The principal public buildings, the Secretariat, the Law Courts, the General Hospital, the Railway Station, are all worthy of the great city which they adorn. The Jail, alas! is one of the most populous in the world. Among buildings deserving special mention is the Roman Catholic cathedral, designed and built by a priest who was an architect and builder of taste and skill. Less conspicuous, but still of sufficient dignity, is the Anglican cathedral.

On the only eminence in or near Rangoon, on a spacious platform, rises the golden splendour of the **Shwe Dagôn Pagoda**, famous among Buddhist shrines, covering relics of the four last Buddhas, the filter or water-strainer of

Krakuchanda, the staff of Kāsyapa, the bathing-robe of Konāgāmana, and eight hairs of Gaudama. Fitch (1586) describes it in glowing words:

It...is of a wonderful bigness, and all gilded from the foot to the top. And there is a house by it wherein the tallipoies, which are their priests, do preach. The house is five and fifty paces in length and has three pawnes, or walks in it, and forty great pillars, gilded, which stand between the walks; and it is

Fig. 67. Shwe Dagôn Pagoda platform.

open on all sides with a number of small pillars, which be likewise gilded. It is gilded with gold within and without. There are houses very fair round about for the pilgrims to lie in, and many goodly houses for the tallipoies to preach in, which are full of images, both of men and women, which are all gilded over with gold. It is the fairest place, as I suppose, that is in the world: it standeth very high, and there are four ways to it, which are all along set with trees of fruits, in such wise that a man may go in shade about two miles in length. And when their feast day is, a man can hardly pass, by water or by land,

Fig. 68. Shwe Dagôn Pagoda platform.

for the great press of people; for they come from all places of the Kingdom of Pegu thither at their feast[1].

The Pagoda consists of a solid mass of brickwork, 312 feet in height from the platform. A great part of the fabric is covered with gold plates renewed from time to time. The whole is crowned by a *ti*, a metal framework studded with jewels, presented by King Mindôn in 1871. The platform

Fig. 69. Shwe Dagôn Pagoda platform.

is crowded with smaller pagodas, *zayats* (rest-houses), *tagundaing* (poles adorned with streamers), subsidiary shrines, and other sacred buildings. Here is a great bell which the British essayed to remove by sea after the Second War. Unluckily, while it was being shipped, it fell into the river and all the king's horses and all the king's men failed to get it up again. In reply to their request,

[1] Hakluyt, II. 393.

the Burmese were told contemptuously that, if they could recover it, they might keep it. So they took a bit of bamboo and fished up the bell and replaced it on the pagoda platform where it still hangs. If you take the deer's horn which lies handy for the purpose, first strike the earth, then strike the bell three times, your wish shall be granted. Approached by a long flight of steps, fringed on either side by rows of stalls where cheroots, toys, candles, and many varieties of miscellaneous goods, are offered for sale, the Pagoda attracts pilgrims and worshippers from all parts of the Province and sigh-seers from distant lands. Any day, one may see pious men and women telling their beads and murmuring their aspirations, acknowledging the misery of this transitory life, burning candles before holy images. As in Fitch's time, on sabbaths and feast days, the platform is crowded with Burmans of all ages, clad in gay silks of many colours, in the best possible temper. The Pagoda is in the custody of trustees who receive the offerings of the faithful and ensure the maintenance in good order of the shrine and its precincts. In too close proximity is an arsenal.

On the border of the city, approximately on the site of King Tharrawaddy's *myo*, lies the cantonment, a wide expanse, including the pagoda, where there are barracks, parade grounds, residences of military and civil officers. Formerly open and picturesque, it is gradually becoming crowded with houses. Presently it will be removed to a distance and the space will be given up to the expansion of the town. On its outskirts, in a well-wooded park, stands Government House, a building of some pretension. Beyond the cantonment lie the Royal Lakes, surrounded by Dalhousie Park, a worthy memorial of the great Governor-General who dedicated it to public use for ever. Nature, skilfully aided by art, has made of its sloping lawns, fairy glades, and winding paths, adorned with flowers in gay and gallant profusion, a scene of almost incomparable beauty.

Rangoon is administered as a separate district. Local affairs are managed by the Municipal Corporation of the City of Rangoon, constituted in 1922 by an elaborate Act recently passed. The Corporation at present consists of 34 Councillors, the maximum number being 40. Of the Councillors, 29 are elected, the rest nominated by the Local Government. Ten are elected by the Burmese community; five by Europeans; four each by Mahomedans and Hindus; two by Chinese; one each by the Port Commissioners, the Chamber of Commerce, the Trades Association, and the Development Trust. The Corporation elects its own President and appoints as its Chief Executive Officer a Commissioner who may be a Government servant. Subject to slight control by the Local Government, the Corporation is empowered to deal exhaustively with all details of municipal administration. The municipal income is about half a million sterling. The town and cantonment are lit by electric light and there is an ample water supply.

One Deputy Commissioner is District Magistrate and controls the administration of criminal justice; a second is Collector. The police of the city is administered by a Commissioner, directly responsible to the Local Government. The rank and file of the police are mostly Indians; but there is a sprinkling of Burmans as well as a small but effective body of mounted European sergeants and constables. The city of Rangoon constitutes a Sessions Division wherein the Chief Court exercises jurisdiction. Trials before the Chief Court are held with the aid of juries, Rangoon and Moulmein, being, except as regards European British subjects, the only places in Burma where the jury system prevails. Large projects for the development of the town are in contemplation. The Rangoon Development Trust, constituted for this purpose, came into being in February, 1921.

Rangoon is the third port in the Indian Empire, surpassed in volume of trade only by Calcutta and Bombay. "Nature has liberally done her part to render Rangoon the most flourishing sea-port of the Eastern world[1]." Much progress has been made in recent years. The whole of the import trade is now conducted alongside modern deep-water wharves lighted by electricity and equipped with hydraulic cranes and spacious sheds. Extensive accommodation has been provided for the inland vessels trade, and the mooring accommodation has been doubled. Some years ago, the existence of the port was in imminent danger. The deep-water channel above Rangoon was being diverted further away from the foreshore on the left bank of the river on which Rangoon stands. At the same time, extensive erosion of the river bed on the left bank threatened to undermine the wharves and jetties. It was decided to build a training wall, two miles long, to force the river back to its former course. This important work was completed early in the year 1914, at the cost of £920,000[2]. The wall is constructed of rubble stone deposited on a foundation of brushwood mattresses; the top consists of slabs of reinforced concrete[3]. The scheme appears to be completely successful.

A project of building an entirely new port at Dawbôn, below the Pazundaung creek, is under consideration. One advantage will be the avoidance of the Hastings shoal, at present a serious impediment to the entrance of the harbour. The new port, if established, will be equipped with docks for which no room can be found in existing circumstances.

In 1921–22, the total value of the sea-borne trade amounted to £89,000,000; to which exports contributed £53,000,000 and imports £36,000,000. The affairs of the port are administered by a Board of Commissioners, most of the members being *ex-officio* or nominated by Government. In 1919–20, the revenue of the port was £523,049, the expenditure £449,593. There was a debt of £2,986,200.

[1] Symes, 217. [2] $Re = 1s. 4d.$
[3] These details are abstracted from accounts by Sir George Buchanan, K.C.I.E., under whose direction the works were executed.

Fig. 70. Moulmein.

Moulmein. Moulmein (61,301)[1], a port of some note, is the oldest British town in Burma, having been established as divisional headquarters in 1827. Situated on the Salween, twenty-eight miles from the sea, within sight of the junction of that river with the Gyaing and Ataran, it commands views of romantic beauty, unsurpassed for picturesque effect[2]. On the ridge above the town are two famous pagodas, Kyaikthanlan (875 A.D.), Uzima or Kyaikpadaw, said to have been built by Asoka. These are celebrated not only for their sanctity but also for the incomparable landscape spread out beneath them. Near Moulmein are well-known caves, haunted by innumerable bats. Commercially and economically, except as the depot of a large timber trade, Moulmein is not of great importance.

Bassein. Bassein (42,503), known to early writers sometimes as Cosmin, sometimes as Persaim, on both sides of the Bassein river, some 60 miles from the sea, is a flourishing port. It was early the seat of a British commercial factory. A centre of the rice trade of the Irrawaddy Delta, it has many rice mills. Bassein is connected with Rangoon by rail, the Irrawaddy being crossed by a ferry at Henzada; and also by a line of river steamers plying through the creeks.

Akyab. Akyab (36,569), the fourth port, is the chief town, and the only town of any size, in the Arakan Division. Built on an island in the Bay of Bengal, in very picturesque surroundings, with an excellent harbour, it is a place of note. Its importance will be greatly enhanced when, in due course, it is connected with India by rail.

Prome. Prome (26,067) stands on the Irrawaddy 161 miles from Rangoon, the northern terminus of the first railway built in Burma. Before the annexation of Upper Burma it was a station on the quickest route to Mandalay. In mediaeval times the capital of a kingdom and the scene of many conflicts, it is now only an ordinary provincial

---

[1] Except where otherwise stated, the figures in brackets give the population according to the census of 1921. [2] See p. 12.

town. It has two famous pagodas, Shwesandaw and Shwe-nattaung. Among the many bells on the platform of Shwesandaw is a beautiful specimen removed by General Godwin in 1852 and after nearly seventy years restored in 1920 by his grandson, Colonel H. H. Godwin-Austen, F.R.S.[1]

Fig. 71. A Burmese family.

Tavoy. Tavoy (27,480), in the Tenasserim Division, on the Tavoy river, is one of the minor ports and the headquarters of a district.

Henzada. Henzada (23,651) on the Irrawaddy is a country town connected with Bassein by rail and with Rangoon by combined river and rail.

[1] The celebrated naturalist and explorer.

Toungoo. Toungoo (19,332), on the Sittaing river, 166 miles from Rangoon, is famous as the early capital of the conqueror, Tabin Shweti. Before the annexation, it was a place of arms on the frontier; and before the building of the railway it was quite remote, the journey to Rangoon occupying many days.

Pegu. Pegu (18,769), on the Pegu river, 47 miles from Rangoon on the railway to Martaban, is a somewhat melancholy relic of ancient splendour. In 1569, in the time of the great King Bayin Naung, it is thus described by Cæsar Frederick:

By the help of God we came safe to Pegu, which are two cities, the old and the new: in the old city are the Merchant strangers, and Merchants of the country, for there are the greatest doings and the greatest trade. This City is not very great, but it hath very great suburbs. Their houses be made with canes and covered with leaves, or with straw; but the Merchants have all one House or Magason, which house they call godon[1], which is made of brickes, and there they put all their goods of any value, to save them from the often mischances that happen to houses made of such stuff. In the new City is the Palace of the King, and his abiding-place with all his barons and nobles and other gentlemen; and in the time I was there they finished building the new city: it is a great City very plain and flat, and four square, walled round about, and with ditches that compass the walls about with water, in which ditches are many Crocodiles. It hath no Drawbridges, yet it hath twenty gates, five for every square; on the walls there are many places made for Sentinels to watch, made of wood, and covered or gilt with gold. The streets thereof are the fairest that I have seen, they are as straight as a line from one gate to another, and standing at one gate you may discern the other, and they are as broad as ten or twelve men may ride abreast in them: and those streets that be thwart are fair and large; these streets both on the one side and the other are planted at the doors of the houses with nut-trees of India, which make a very commodious shadow: the houses be made of wood, and covered with a kind of tiles in form of cups, very necessary for

---

[1] *Godown*, a store room, is a word still commonly used.

their use. The King's Palace is in the middle of the city, made
in form of a walled castle with ditches full of water round about
it; the lodgings within are made of wood all over gilded, with
fine pinnacles, and very costly work, covered with plates of
gold. Truly it may be a King's house: within the gate there is
a fair large Court, from the
one side to the other wherein
there are made places for the
strongest and stoutest elephants appointed for the
service of the King's person,
and amongst all other elephants he has four that be
white, a thing so rare that a
man shall hardly find another
King that has any such, and
if the King know that any
other hath white elephants,
he sendeth for them as for a
gift[1].

Now Pegu is a small pro-
vincial town, chiefly interesting on account of its rich
treasures of Buddhist an-
tiquities. Conspicuous are

Fig. 72. Burman at his
devotions.

the beautiful Shwemawdaw Pagoda, 324 feet in height,
dating from the 6th century; vividly described by Captain
Symes; and the great recumbent image of Gaudama
Buddha called the Shin-bin-tha-lyaung.

Mergui. Mergui (17,297), on the Tenasserim coast, was
formerly classed with Rangoon and Negrais as one of the
three best ports in the east[2]. Crawfurd writes: "The best
and securest harbour, without reference, however, to commercial convenience is that of Mergui....This will admit
vessels of almost any burthen, and the ingress and egress
are perfectly safe at all times[3]." Mergui is the depot of

[1] Hakluyt, II. 362.   [2] Symes.
[3] Crawfurd, 478.

the pearling industry and has some trade in tin, but is otherwise undistinguished. Notwithstanding its natural advantages, its value as a port is small as it leads nowhither and has no hinterland.

Thatôn. Thatôn (15,091), an inland town in the Tenasserim division, was formerly a Talaing capital and also a seaport. Anawrata destoyed it in the 11th century, and the retrogression of the sea has long left it high and dry. It is on the railway line between Rangoon and Martaban.

Insein. Insein (14,308) is a flourishing and rising railway town, ten miles from Rangoon. Near it are the golf links of Mingaladôn, said to be almost the best course in the East.

Yandoon. Yandoon (12,500)[1], at the junction of the Irrawaddy and the Panlang creek, 60 miles from Rangoon, was formerly a trading town of some importance. It is now one of the few towns with a dwindling population.

Paungdè. Paungdè (14,154) is a railway town in the Prome district, 130 miles from Rangoon.

Thayetmyo. Thayetmyo (10,768), "the city of slaughter," is on the Irrawaddy, a few miles below the old frontier of Upper Burma. Formerly, it was strongly garrisoned, but since the annexation it has sunk into comparative insignificance.

Syriam. Syriam (15,193), not far from Rangoon, was once a provincial capital and, as already noted, the seat of the earliest commercial settlements. It has grown rapidly in recent years, its population in 1891 being under 2000. Now it is the centre of a thriving oil-refining industry.

UPPER BURMA

Mandalay. In the year 1857, Mindôn Min, following the traditional custom of his House when the throne was filled otherwise than by regular succession, decreed the removal of his court from Amarapura to Mandalay where, in consequence, a populous town arose. The new capital was

[1] In 1911.

occupied in 1859. The site chosen was on the left bank of the Irrawaddy, in latitude 20° 59′ N., at a place convenient as a centre of trade with the Northern Shan country. It is not clear that it had any other advantage.

The present town, city, and cantonment occupy an area of 25 square miles. In 1885, Mandalay was the most populous city in Burma, and so it remained for a few years,

Fig. 73. South Moat Gate, Mandalay.

the population in 1891 being returned at 188,815, while that of Rangoon was only 182,080. By 1911, the inhabitants of Mandalay had fallen to 138,299. But in the next ten years there was a revival and the number is now 148,917. Mandalay is still essentially a Burmese town, the Buddhist element largely prevailing. Situated 386 miles from Rangoon it is connected with the capital of the province by rail and by river.

The type of Burmese royal city has remained unaltered

for ages. Cæsar Frederick's description of Pegu[1] might be adopted almost word for word for Mandalay, save that there were no crocodiles in the moat and there was no ditch round the palace. The commercial and trading quarters extend along the river bank without a break to Amarapura. This low-lying area is protected from inundation by a double embankment built partly for that purpose and partly as a safeguard against hostile attack from the river. In 1886, at the height of the rains, the embankment gave way and the water poured through, flooding the lower part of the town. Boats and launches plied as far as the Zegyo, the great bazaar. In 1885, most of the houses were flimsy structures of wood and bamboo. The greater number of these were destroyed by frequent fires which raged at the end of the hot weather of the following year. Now there are many masonry buildings. Although not a commercial centre of importance, all industries characteristic of the country are practised at Mandalay. A specially flourishing trade is the making of sacred images in marble and steatite. In the middle of the town is the Zegyo, one of the finest covered bazaars in the East, where silks and jewels and miscellaneous goods are displayed in lavish abundance.

Some three miles from the river, stands the *Myo* or city, encompassed by a moat, 225 feet wide, once covered with lilies, and by battlemented walls, 27 feet high. Each face of the square enclosure is about a mile and a quarter in length. The walls are pierced by twelve gates, each approached by a bridge over the moat, and each surmounted by a *pyathat* or terraced spire, not used, I think, as sentry boxes. Between these are studded other *pyathats* making forty-eight in all. One of these surmounts Government House which, being designed in Burmese style, does not outrage aesthetic sensibility. In the middle of the square still stands the Palace. When Mandalay was occupied in 1885, the area around the Palace was crowded with houses

[1] See p. 182.

of ministers, officers of State, and other Government servants (*ahmudan*). Each of the more important mansions,
mostly built of timber, stood in the midst of its own *win*,
compound, or garden. After the occupation the walled city
became a place of arms, the main part of the cantonment
which was named Fort Dufferin to commemorate the
Governor-General by whom Upper Burma was added to
the Empire. In process of time, the whole of the land within

Fig. 74. Between wall and moat, Mandalay.

the walls was acquired by Government and all the inhabitants were compensated and expropriated. The space thus
cleared was filled with barracks, parade grounds, recreation fields, houses of military and civil officers; and so it
remains to this day.

The palace of King Mindôn and King Thebaw was built
so recently as 1845 by Shwebo Min and was transported
bodily from Amarapura to Mandalay. It was surrounded
by a teak wood stockade and two inner encircling walls.

On a raised masonry and boarded platform was piled an irregular maze of buildings, mostly in Burmese style, but mingled with some of modern design. East and west, with gilded roofs upheld by lofty pillars of teak, were spacious audience halls, each with its golden throne; for the most exalted ceremonies, in the east, the Lion Throne; in the west, where the ladies of the court paid obeisance, the Lily Throne. Seven other thrones were used on various occasions. Towering above the eastern hall was the famous tapering nine-storeyed spire. Between the two halls were the royal apartments, quarters for princes and princesses, courtiers, maids of honour and pages, offices for ministers, the State Theatre, the Treasury. At the south-eastern corner stood a wooden tower of recent date. Near the eastern gate, beyond the outer wall, was the turret on which was placed the *bohozin*, the great drum sounded to mark the hours and to give assurance that the king was in his palace. Between the inner wall and the main building stood a small gilded monastery and opposite it the *Hlutdaw* or Council Chamber where also was the Record Office. Not far away[1] was the shed of the white elephant[1]. The ornamentation of the buildings on the platform was tawdry and barbaric; even the wood-carving was not of special distinction. As a whole, the palace is more curious and interesting than beautiful. But the central *pyathat* is a model of grace and the pillared halls have a majestic dignity.

Within the enclosure, like Kubla Khan's pleasure-dome, the palace was surrounded by lovely gardens, bright with sinuous rills, where blossomed many an incense-bearing tree and gorgeous tropical flowers, with here a graceful bridge, there a gay pavilion. Here was the summer house where King Thebaw surrendered to General Prendergast. Afterwards this little house acquired even a better title to respect as the temporary abode of Lord Roberts. It has now disappeared.

[1] This loyal beast declined to survive the downfall of his sovereign.

The palace has been carefully preserved. At first, after the occupation, it was filled with offices and quarters; the western hall became a club house, the eastern hall a church.

Fig. 75. The Palace Gardens.

Club and church have long since been evicted as well as all residents; and now the lizard and the swarthy *darwan*[1] keep the empty halls where King Thebaw rioted and revelled. The stockade has been replaced by neat post and rails.

[1] Watchman.

The *Hlutdaw* has crumbled away. But most of the buildings
on the platform still stand as in the time of the Burmese
monarchy.

To the north is Mandalay Hill, 950 feet high, whereon
stood an upright image of the Buddha, with arm out-
stretched, the Palladium of the city. The image, destroyed
by fire some years ago, has been replaced. On a spur of
the hill has been built a temple to receive relics of Gaudama
recovered from a pagoda near Peshawar erected by the
Emperor Kanishka. East are the Shan Hills and in the
middle distance the isolated little hill of Yankintaung, the
hill of peace.

Mandalay is studded with pagodas and monasteries, for
the most part modern. South of the town is the **Arakan
Pagoda** or rather Temple (*Yakaing Paya*), enshrining the
great Mahamuni image, cast in the second century of our
era, and brought from Arakan in 1784. Here also are six
antique and much dilapidated bronze images, two men,
three lions, and a three-headed elephant. The corridors
leading to the shrine are adorned with frescoes. In a small
lake or pond are tame tortoises fed by the pious. Here,
for the present, are kept the relics from Peshawar.

Some other pagodas may be mentioned. Kyauktawgyi
covers an image of the Buddha made in marble under the
orders of Mindôn Min. At Sandemani are the graves of the
Einshemin (heir apparent), and the Sagu and Malun princes,
killed in the abortive rising of the Myingun prince in 1866.
Kuthodaw, not far from the foot of Mandalay Hill, is one
of the most remarkable. In the midst is a graceful pagoda;
around it are 729 stone slabs on which are inscribed the
whole of the *Tripataka* or Buddhist scriptures. Setkyathila
covers a bronze image of the Buddha cast under the orders
of King Bagyidaw. One of the finest specimens of Burmese
art, the image is somewhat fancifully regarded as of sinister
omen. Its casting at Ava in 1823 was followed by the First
War in 1824; its removal to Amarapura in 1849 by the

Second War in 1852; its final transfer to Mandalay in 1884 by the Third War in the following year. Eindawya, built by Pagan Min in 1847, is of conspicuous merit; Menaung Yawana, built in 1881, may commemorate King Thebaw. The Atumashi, or Incomparable, a large and beautiful temple covered with white stucco, enshrining a great image of the Buddha, was destroyed by fire in 1890. Paya-ni, the Red Pagoda, dates from 1092. Attached to it are two

Fig. 76. Queens' Monastery, Mandalay.

images, Naungdaw and Nyidaw, of the time of Anawrata. In its present form, Shwekyimyin dates only from 1852 but was superimposed on an old pagoda of 1104. It covers a great brazen image of Gaudama as well as other sacred images, notably one, Shwelinbin, representing Gaudama in royal robes, said to have been moved from capital to capital since the time of King Narapati-sithu of Pagan (11th century). A small nameless pagoda was built by Shinbome, a famous beauty, who, with the necessary variation almost equalling the exploits of Henry VIII, married five kings in succession.

Many monasteries, built by kings, queens and courtiers, adorn the town. The best known is the Queen's Monastery, finished by Supayalat just before the Third War. At the time of the annexation its gold was fresh and gleaming. Shwenandaw, built by King Thebaw in 1880, and Salin, by Salin Supaya, a favourite child of Mindôn Min, daughter of the Limban queen, as well as the Queen's Monastery, are all remarkable for beautiful wood-carving, that on Salin being probably the finest in Burma. Sangyaung was built in 1859 by Mindôn Min. Taiktaw is the official residence of the Thathanabaing[1].

Pakôkku. Pakôkku (19,507), on the right bank of the Irrawaddy, near its junction with the Chindwin, is described by Crawfurd as

"a place of considerable extent and population. The inhabitants" he writes "poured out on the banks to see the steam-vessel, and formed such a concourse as we had nowhere seen unless at Prome. [Pakôkku] is a place of great trade, and a kind of emporium for the commerce between Ava and the lower country; many large boats which cannot proceed to the former in the dry season, taking in their cargoes at this place. We counted one hundred and fifty trading vessels, of which twenty one were of the largest size of Burman merchant-boats[2]."

But in 1889 the population was estimated at no more than 8000. Since then Pakôkku has thriven and is now again a busy industrial and trading centre and an important timber depot.

Myingyan. Myingyan (18,931), on the left bank of the Irrawaddy, about 80 miles below Mandalay, connected by a branch line from Thazi with the Rangoon-Mandalay railway, is an industrial and trading town of some note, the seat of busy cotton mills. It suffers from being cut off from the river in the dry season by sandbanks.

[1] See p. 128.   [2] Crawfurd, 74.

Pyinmana. Pyinmana (14,886), on the Mandalay railway, 226 miles from Rangoon, derives its importance from its proximity to valuable teak forests. It was one of the first inland towns occupied at the time of the invasion of Upper Burma in 1885.

Maymyo. Maymyo (16,558), already mentioned as the summer capital, is situated on the border of the Shan sub-State of Hsum-sai[1] (Thonze), east of Mandalay, on a wide plateau some 3500 feet above the sea. Built on the site of the village of Pyin-u-lwin and named after its first Commandant, Colonel May of the Indian army, Maymyo owes its prosperity entirely to British occupation. When first visited towards the end of 1886, Pyin-u-lwin consisted of about fifty houses, a monastery, a market place, and a gambling ring. Now the railway from Mandalay to Lashio passes through it and there is also connection with Mandalay by a good motor road. Besides being the seat of Government in the hot season, it is the military head-quarters of Burma, and the resort of many visitors from the plains. There is ample room for a race-course, golf links, polo, cricket and football grounds, a club, barracks, private houses with delicious gardens, and public offices. Carriage drives and good roads for motoring have been laid out. To Sir Hugh Barnes, the second Lieutenant-Governor, is due the provision of some 60 miles of rough rides through the forest on the outskirts. Maymyo is singularly unlike typical eastern places; it has been described as more like a corner of Surrey. The only conspicuous native feature is the bazaar or market, held after Shan fashion every five days, where strange people from the hills in picturesque attire mingle with Europeans and Shans and Burmans.

Mogôk. Mogôk (11,069)[2] was from 1887 to 1920 the head-quarters of the Ruby Mines district, recently absorbed into Katha. Picturesquely situated amid lofty hills, at an elevation of about 4000 feet, connected with the Irrawaddy at

---

[1] Absorbed in Hsipaw.   [2] In 1911.

Thabeik-kyin by a motor road 60 miles in length, it is important solely as the centre of the ruby mining industry. It has always been a wealthy town where, in the bazaar

Fig. 77. Mingun Pagoda.

in 1887, copper coins were unknown. A few miles away, at a greater height, is Bernard-myo, commemorating Sir Charles Bernard, the distinguished officer who was the first Chief Commissioner in Upper Burma.

Sagaing. Sagaing (11,737), one of many ancient capitals, is a typical Burmese town, embowered in tamarind groves, on the right bank of the Irrawaddy a few miles below Mandalay. It is the southern terminus of the railway to Myit-kyi-na and is also connected by rail with Mônywa and Alôn on the Chindwin. From Mandalay, a steam ferry plies several times a day in connection with the railway. Except as the headquarters of a Division and District, Sagaing has no special importance but it has many associations and notable neighbours. Nearly opposite on the left bank of the river stood the ancient and famous city of Ava, now in ruin and decay. A little to the north is the great bell of Mingun, the largest hung bell in the world. Cast in 1790, it weighs 80 tons, with a height of 12 feet and a diameter at the mouth of 16 feet. It was re-hung a few years ago. Close by, at Mingun, is a vast uncompleted pagoda planned by Bodawpaya to be of unapproached dimensions, but abandoned after it had been split by an earthquake in 1839. With a base of 450 feet square and height of 162 feet, it enjoys the unromantic distinction of being the greatest mass of solid brick work extant. Hard by is Sinbyushin, a beautiful terraced pagoda, dating from the 14th century. To the north the hills along the river are crowned with white pagodas in picturesque disorder; hollowed out of the hills are cave dwellings of hermits.

Shwebo. Shwebo (10,605), an inland town on the Myit-kyina railway, is noted as the birth-place of Alaungpaya and the capital of his kingdom. Traces of the royal city still remain. In Burmese times Shwebo was often the seed-plot of rebellion.

Bhamo. Bhamo (7741), an ancient town on the left bank of the Irrawaddy, 687 miles from the sea, is an emporium of the caravan trade with China. It is one of the places to which European traders first penetrated. Among its inhabitants are a fair sprinkling of Chinese from Yünnan and some from Canton; its most conspicuous building is an elaborately ornamented Chinese temple Bhamo is important as a frontier garrison town, having been occupied immediately after the taking of Mandalay.

Amarapura. Amarapura (7866)[1], a decaying town, practically a suburb of Mandalay, is chiefly notable as a former

capital. It still has some economic importance, with an exceedingly useful silk-weaving institute and with many carvers of images. Here used to be the *kheddah*, the enclosure into which wild elephants were enticed in the king's time and in our early years. Here are many famous pagodas; the Shwegyetyet group, 600 years old; Pato-dawgyi, a very large and beautiful pagoda decorated with glazed tiles, the work of King Bagyidaw in 1818; and Kyauktawgyi built by

Fig. 78. Shrine at Amarapura.

Pagan Min in 1847 on the model of the Ananda at Pagan, its porches adorned with frescoes.

Pagan. Pagan (6254)[2], on the left bank of the Irrawaddy, below Myingyan, is one of the most remarkable places in the world. The most renowned of ancient Burmese capitals, it is still a wonder-house of archaeological relics. So long ago as the 2nd century of our era, a city was built on this site. But Pagan, of which the ruins are extant, was founded by King Pyinbya in 847 A.D. In 1057 Anawrata, most renowned of Burmese kings, destroyed the kingdom of Thatôn and brought to his capital King Manuha and many Talaing captives. From this date begins the epoch of pagoda-building at Pagan, lasting till the sack of the city by the Mongols and Chinese of Kublai Khan in 1284, and

[1] In 1911.   [2] In 1901.

embracing the reigns of Anawrata, Kyansittha, Alaung-sithu, Narapati-sithu, and Talokpye Min. For miles along the river bank are still standing some 5000 pagodas and Buddhist temples, Pagan itself extending for five miles with a breadth of two miles; but the area occupied by sacred buildings at Pagan and in the vicinity is about 100 square miles[1]. Shortly before the Mongol invasion, Marco Polo describes Pagan which he calls Amien, the capital city of the province of that name, as "a very great and noble city[2]."

"And in this city," he writes, "there is a thing so rich and rare that I must tell you about it. You see there was in former days a rich and puissant King in this city and when he was about to die he commanded that by his tomb they should erect two towers (one at each end), one of gold and the other of silver, in such fashion as I shall tell you. The towers are built of fine stone; and the one of them has been covered with gold, a good finger in thickness, so that the tower looks as if it were all of solid gold; and the other is covered with silver in like manner so that it seems to be all of solid silver. Each tower is of a good ten paces in height and of breadth in proportion. The Upper Part of these towers is round, and girt all along with bells, the top of the gold tower with gilded bells and the silver tower with silvered bells, insomuch that whenever the wind blows among these bells they tinkle. The King caused these towers to be erected to commemorate his magnificence and for the good of his soul, and really they do form one of the finest sights in the world; so exquisitely finished are they, so splendid and costly."

Unhappily no remains of these exquisite buildings can be traced, but many worthy compeers survive. In the classical description of the antiquities of Pagan, Sir Henry Yule thus summarizes the several styles of architecture:

The bell-shaped pyramid of dead brickwork in all its varieties; the same raised over a square or octagonal cell, containing an image of the Buddha; the bluff, knob-like dome of the Ceylon Dagobahs, with the square cap which seems to have charac-

[1] Taw Sein Ko, C.I.E. *Archaeological Notes on Pagan.*
[2] Marco Polo, II. 109.

terized the most ancient Buddhist chaityas, as represented in
the sculptures at Sanchi, and in the ancient model pagodas
found near Buddhist remains in India; the fantastic boo-payah,
or pumpkin pagoda, which seemed rather like a fragment of
what we might conceive the architecture of the moon than
anything terrestrial, and many variations of these types. But
the predominant and characteristic form is that of the cruciform
vaulted temple[1].

Ananda. The most famous temple is the Ananda, of Jain
architecture, with vaulted chambers and corridors, built
in the year 1091 and still standing almost untouched by
time. It contains stone sculptures representing scenes of
Gaudama's life and terra cotta tiles picturing events of his
former existences, as well as images of the founder King
Kyansittha and of the last four Buddhas of the present
cycle.

Tha-byin-nyu, another magnificent temple, built by
Alaung-sithu in 1244 after models of temples in Northern
India, is thus described:

...The form of the temple is an equilateral quadrangle,
having on each side four large wings, also of a quadrilateral
form. In these last are the entrances, and they contain the
principal images of Gautama. Each side of the temple measures
about two hundred and thirty feet. The whole consists of four
stages, or stories, diminishing in size as they ascend. The ground
story only has wings. The centre of the building consists of a
solid mass of masonry: over this, and rising from the last story
of the building, is a steeple, in form not unlike a mitre, ending
in a thin spire, which is crowned with an iron umbrella, as in
the modern temples. Round each stage of the building is an
arched corridor, and on one side a flight of steps leads all the
way to the last story....Perhaps the most remarkable feature
of this temple, as well as of almost all the other buildings of
Pagan, is the prevalence of the arch. The gate ways, the doors,
the galleries, and the roofs of all the smaller temples, are invariably formed by a well-turned Gothic arch[2].

Other notable temples of Indian types and giving evidence
of Indian influence are Maha Bodi, a copy of the shrine at

---

[1] *The Court of Ava*, 35.   [2] Crawfurd, 63–4.

Fig. 79. Ananda (Pagan).

Buddha Gaya in Bengal and Gawdapalin, built by Nara-pati-sithu in the 12th century. Of a small unnamed temple, Crawfurd writes: "within the chamber were two good images in sandstone, and sculptured in high relief. One of these was Vishnu or Krishna, sitting on his *Garuda*; and the other Siwa, the destroying power, with his *trisula*, or trident, in one hand and a mallet in the other[1]." The first temple built by Anawrata enshrines hairs of the Buddha; the corners of the lowest terrace are guarded by images of Brahma, Vishnu, and Siwa.

Specially deserving of mention are Shwegugyi, built by Alaungsithu in the 12th century; Tilomile, a two-storeyed building, dating from 1218; and Shwezigôn, one of the oldest buildings in Pagan.

A few hundred yards South of [Shwezigôn] lies ensconced amid green verdure and ruins, Kyansittha's *Ônhmin* or the Cave Temple of King Kyansittha (1084–1112 A.D.). It is a brick building of unpretentious dimensions, and is almost hidden from view because its site has been scooped out of a sand-dune. As the Ananda temple is the store-house of the finest statuary in stone in Burma, so this Cave Temple contains the best collection of exquisite frescoes illustrating Burmese civilization, probably before the 11th century A.D. Such Cave Temples are numerous in the neighbourhood[2].

Dhammayazaka temple, built by King Narapatisithu, 1196, contains images of the five Buddhas of the present cycle including Arimetteyya who is still to appear.

Besides temples and pagodas, many in good preservation, ruined monasteries abound in great numbers and of various types[3]. Enough has been cited to indicate the extreme wealth of Pagan in archaeological treasures to the examination of which much labour has been devoted in recent years.

The flourishing and unique lacquer industry has already been described.

---

[1] Crawfurd, 69.   [2] Taw Sein Ko, *Burmese Sketches*, II. 303.
[3] Cf. Captain W. B. Sinclair's "The Monasteries of Pagan." *Journal of the Burma Research Society*, X. i.

CHAPTER XX

ARCHITECTURE AND ANTIQUITIES

ALL that is characteristic in Burmese architecture is embodied in buildings sacred to the Buddhist religion. Except the palace at Mandalay, there were, in recent Burmese times, literally no secular buildings of beauty, grandeur, or importance. The houses of even the highest officers of State were wooden structures, raised from the ground on wooden posts, situated in the midst of a spacious *win* (compound or enclosure) in which around the central buildings were scattered the smaller houses of retainers. Humbler dwellings, in town or village, were of similar type and in rural parts these conditions still prevail. In towns a good many masonry houses have been built. In Mandalay, there were some of these, but not many, in Burmese times.

Pagodas. Pagodas abound all over the country. The typical Burmese pagoda is well described by the early traveller, Fitch:

They be made round like a sugar loaf; some are as high as a church, very broad beneath; some a quarter of a mile in compass; within they be all earth, done about with stone...they be all gilded aloft; and many of them from the top to the bottom; and every ten or twelve years they must be new gilded, because the rain consumeth off the gold; for they stand open abroad[1].

The description holds good in the present day. But the great majority of pagodas, elsewhere than in large towns, are not gilded but simply covered with white stucco. Every village has its pagoda; and many are built in waste places, and on the tops of hills. The supreme work of merit is the building of a pagoda; the highest unofficial title of respect, *paya-taga*, pagoda-builder. The more pretentious pagodas

---

[1] Hakluyt, II. 393.

are built on raised platforms whereon are crowded shrines, *zayats* (rest-houses), images, altars for lights and flowers, bells, *tagundaing* (posts decorated with streamers), water-stands, images of the Buddha.

Pagodas at Rangoon, Mandalay, Pagan, and elsewhere have already been described. A long list of other pagodas might be compiled and an account of Burma would be incomplete without mention of the most notable. When great

Fig. 80. Chinthes, figures at Pagoda entrance.

age is assigned to a pagoda, it must not be supposed that it was built originally of its present height and splendour. The first building was probably small and insignificant, magnified by later accretions superimposed.

In the midst of Rangoon stands the Sule Pagoda, of venerable antiquity, but overshadowed by the dominance of Shwe Dagôn. In Thatôn are Zingyaik (11th century) and a pagoda said to have been built by King Dhammacheti in the 15th century; and at Kyaikkatha in that district are the remains of a thousand pagodas.

Most famous among the small pagodas is the **Kyaik-htee-yoh**[1] insignificant in size, but unique from its position. The hill on which it stands takes its name from the payah, and is over three thousand five hundred feet in height. On its summit are numbers of granitoid boulders, many of them balanced in

Fig. 81. Pagodas at Sagaing.

a most extraordinary way, and all the more striking surmounted by little shrines. The Kyaik-htee-yoh stands on a huge boulder, which itself rests on a projecting rock, separated from the rest of the hills by a chasm, fathomless to the eye, and reaching, so say the villagers, far below the depth of the hill. The boulder hangs on the extreme verge of the bare rock, and hangs over it as if a gust of wind or a few extra pounds added would make it topple over and crash down the giddy height far away into the green valley below. To this shrine people from all parts of

[1] Also in the Thatôn district.

the country but more especially the Talaings, come in the month of February, and cast jewellery and precious stones into the yawning rift, and, clambering up the rock by the aid of a bamboo ladder, cover the payah with flowers and small lighted candles, making it look like a new nebulous constellation from the far off plains. Inquirers are told with the utmost confidence that the pagoda is five thousand years old. It certainly has been there time out of mind, and the boulder has solely been kept in its place by the hair buried under the shrine, and given to a hermit by the great Budh himself when he returned from Tawa-dehutha, the second heaven of the Nat-dewahs, on the occasion of his preaching the law to his mother....The view from the pagoda is superb; bounded on the east by the blue Martaban hills, fading away into the dim peaks of Siam; and extending southward over tangled jungle and yellow paddy lands to the bright waves of the Gulf of Martaban, while to the west the jewelled speck of the pagoda at Pegu almost leads one to imagine the stately bulk of the Shway Dagohn beyond[1].

Bilugyun in Amherst has sixty pagodas of venerable age. At Amherst Point is Yele, within a hundred feet of which no woman may tread. Sandaw, in the same district, claims to be as old as Shwe Dagôn. At a very famous pagoda, Shin-môkti, in Tavoy, is an image which floated miraculously across the Bay of Bengal. Other shrines of great antiquity in Tavoy and Mergui are merely names.

In Arakan, the most interesting archaeological remains are at Mrohaung, the capital from 1430 to 1782.

The largest and best monuments and sculptures of Mrohaung belong to the 15th and 16th centuries. Their interest lies in the fact that some of them are unlike in style to anything seen in the rest of Burma; they were temples as well as forts at the same time. Another interesting feature, very rare in Burma, and even in Pagan itself, is that stone was very largely used for building....Solid or cylindrical pagodas...are completely built of stone and are generally among the best preserved monuments at Mrohaung[2].

---

[1] *The Burman*, 167–168.
[2] *Archaeological Survey Report*, Burma, 1920–21.

In the architecture as well as in the subjects of some of the stone carvings are many traces of Hindu influence.

The Shittaung temple, with its hundred images of Buddha, the Dakkan-thein, a temple fortress, the An-daw or Tooth-relic Temple, the Ratanabon Pagoda, a quaint structure of the solid cylindrical type, the Lemyethna Temple, the Rata-man-aung Pagoda[1]

are among the principal shrines. At Vesālī, the site of a

Fig. 82. Turtle tank, Arakan Pagoda.

more ancient capital, near Mrohaung, are also interesting relics.

Thayetmyo has Shwemyindin or Shwe-sut-taung-byi (the golden shrine of prayers granted) dating from the first century of our era. Shwezettaw (the golden footprint) in Minbu commemorates a visit of Gaudama Buddha. Anawrata is reputed to have built Taung-gyi-swe-daw opposite Pagan and Sut-taung-byi in Madaya (Mandalay district), the latter to celebrate victories over China. Shwezayun, on the Myitngè, is famous for its tame fish which come for

[1] *Archaeological Survey Report, ut sup.*

food when called and are decorated with gold leaf by visitors at the pagoda festival. In Sagaing is the celebrated **Kaunghmudaw**, built by Thalun Mintayagyi, King of Ava, in 1636. Two others date from the 10th century. In Kyauksè, Asoka built at least one and Anawrata many pagodas which still exist; and here is Shwemôktaw, built

Fig. 83. Eindawya Pagoda.

by a king more than two thousand years ago. Meiktila has two pagodas of Anawrata and of Narapatisithu. An interesting shrine in Myingyan is Kyauk-ku, the rock-cave pagoda, under and near which are caves where hermits dwell. Shwegu near Bhamo, "is a perfect forest of Pagodas[1]."

[1] *The Burman*, 174.

In the Shan States are many renowned pagodas; among which may be mentioned Mwedaw at Bawgyo in Hsipaw; Kaunghmu Mwedaw Manloi in South Hsenwi, built on the spot where Gaudama died in one of his earlier incarnations as a parrot; Kaunghmu Kawmong at Manhpai, illuminated by nats on dark nights; Anteng and Thandaung in Yawnghwe said to have been built by Asoka and repaired by Anawrata.

Fig. 84. Thein.

Besides pagodas, Burmese sacred buildings include monasteries, *thein*[1], and *zayat*[2]. Some of the more notable monasteries have already been described. Every village has its monastery, a one-storeyed building, where the monk and his acolytes reside, absorbed in meditation or engaged in teaching young boys.

Inscriptions. "Burma is one of the very richest countries in Indo-China in lithic inscriptions. The least religious

[1] Halls for the ordination of monks.
[2] Rest-houses for travellers and pilgrims.

foundation, benefaction, or dedication of land, slaves, or fruit trees was generally recorded on stone." But hardly any inscriptions have been found earlier than the middle of the 11th century A.D.[1]

Images. Some famous images have been mentioned. At Păgăt, on the Salween, is a notable collection. Here are the famous caves where besides countless numbers at the entrance are myriads of statues within.

In the words of a bye-gone traveller:—"(The cave) is of vast size, chiefly in one apartment, which needs no human art to render it sublime. The eye is confused, and the heart appalled....Everywhere, on the floor, overhead, on the jutting points, and on the stalactite festoons of the roof, are crowded together images of Gautama—the offerings of successive ages. Some are perfectly gilded; others encrusted with calcareous matter; some fallen, yet sound; others mouldered; others just erected. Some of these are of stupendous size; some not larger than one's finger; and some of all the intermediate sizes—marble, stone, wood, brick, and clay. Some even of marble, are so time-worn though sheltered from change of temperature, that the face and fingers are obliterated. Here and there are models of temples, *kyoungs*[2], etc., some not larger than half a bushel, and some ten or fifteen feet square, absolutely filled with small idols, heaped promiscuously one on the other. As we followed the path, which wound among the groups of figures and models, every new aspect of the cave presented new multitudes of images[3]."

Another remarkable group exists at Akauktaung, on the edge of the Irrawaddy, at the extreme north of the Henzada district.

Here the right bank rises proudly to a lofty cliff, overhung with evergreen forest, and this cliff is made holy and glorious by hundreds and hundreds of images of the Buddha, each in its separate shrine, sculptured tier above tier out of the solid rock. The Buddhas sit royally enthroned, a splendid company, looking

[1] *Archaeological Survey Report, ut sup.*
[2] *Kyaung*, a monastery.
[3] Cited from a chapter of *The Silken East* (XXXIII.), which contains an admirable description of the caves and their vicinity.

down upon the river, watching the great steamers pass and little canoes freighted with laughing children; listening to the song of the Irrawaddy and to the little bells on the tiny white pagoda on the edge of the cliff. Transfigured in sunlight, the Buddhas glow in their dark frame of forest, under shimmering daylight skies. Radiant, unearthly, they gleam in the witchery of Eastern moonlight.

Fig. 85. Gaudama Buddha.

It seems as if the whole wonderful group must have arisen in a single moment at the bidding of a divinity, so ethereal, so harmonious is the impression it makes upon the mind. Yet each image owes its existence to the piety of some simple husband-man, spending with royal largesse the proceeds of his harvest. The Burman, no wise calculator, gives all he can and knows not ignoble thrift[1].

[1] Marjorie Laurie.

BIBLIOGRAPHY

Reports

General Administration.
Upper Burma Administration (1886).
Archaeological Survey.
Myaungmya Settlement (1916–1919).
Sagaing Settlement (1915–1918).
Trade and Navigation.
Maritime Trade and Customs.
Overland Trade.
Census (1911).

Gazetteers

Imperial Gazetteer of India—Burma.
Upper Burma. Sir George Scott.
Chin Hills. Sir B. S. Carey and Mr H. N. Tuck.
Myitkyina District. Mr W. A. Hertz.

Marco Polo. Ed. Yule and Cordier.
Hakluyt's Voyages. Ed. 1810.
Embassy to the Court of Ava (1795). Captain M. Symes.
Embassy to the Court of Ava (1827). J. Crawfurd.
Mission to the Court of Ava (1855). Sir Henry Yule.
History of Burma. Sir Arthur Phayre.
The Pacification of Burma. Sir Charles Crosthwaite.
Our Burmese Wars. Colonel W. F. B. Laurie.
The Story of Burma. Mr G. G. Harmer.
The Burman. Shway Yoe (Sir George Scott).
The Burmese Empire. Father Sangermano.
Burma under British Rule. J. Nisbet.
Burma. Mr E. H. Parker.
The Soul of a People. H. Fielding.
The Silken East. Mr V. C. Scott O'Connor.
Mandalay, etc. Mr V. C. Scott O'Connor.
In Farthest Burma. Captain Kingdon Ward.
Burmese Sketches. Mr Taw Sein Ko.
Journal of the Burma Research Society.
L'Architecture Hindoueen Extrême—Orient. General L. de Beylie.
Le Tibete Revolte. J. Bacot (translation).
Shans at Home. Mrs Leslie Milne.
Fauna of British India.
Poisonous Snakes of India. Sir Joseph Fayrer.
Report on Fisheries. Colonel F. D. Maxwell.

Adventure, Sport and Travel, on Tibetan Steppes. W. N. Fergusson.
Big game shooting in Upper Burma. Colonel G. H. Evans.
Game animals of India. R. Lyddeker.
Birds of British Burma. E. W. Oates.
Journal of the Bombay Natural History Society (Vol. VII).
Flora of British Burma. Kurz.
Handbook of Forest products of Burma. Mr A. Rodger.
Journal of the Linnaean Society (Vol. XXVIII).
Records of the Botanical Survey of India (Vol. III).
The Commercial Products of India. Sir George Watt.
The Sea-Gypsies of Malaya. Walter Grainge White.
A Civil Servant in Burma.

APPENDIX I

AVERAGE ANNUAL RAINFALL FROM 1917 TO 1920 (INCLUSIVE)

(See pp. 16–19)

Mergui	...	...	... 149·03.	1920	Palaw	279·17
Tavoy	...	...	... 217·65			
Moulmein	...	...	... 204·03			
Thatôn	...	...	... 214·62			
Toungoo	...	...	... 81·40	1920	{Thandaung	184·20
					{Yedashe	47·17
Papun	...	...	... 113·41			
Pegu	...	...	... 125·42			
Rangoon	...	...	... 94·61			
Insein	...	...	... 87·15			
Hanthawaddy (Kyauktan)			111·34			
Tharrawaddy	...	...	84·83			
Prome	...	...	... 43·00			
Maubin	...	...	... 97·92			
Pyapôn	...	...	... 94·18			
Bassein	...	...	... 103·87			
Myaungmya	...	...	96·33			
Henzada	...	...	... 84·32			
Thayetmyo	...	...	45·79			
Magwe	...	...	... 28·78			
Minbu	...	...	... 34·71			
Pakôkku	...	...	... 20·66.	1920	Gangaw	52·63
Kampetlet	...	...	... 93·09			
Yamèthin	...	...	33·52;	1920,	23·69	
Pyinmana	...	...	40·47			
Meiktila	...	...	... 32·34			
Myingyan	...	...	29·25;	1920,	23·95	
Kyauksè	...	...	... 32·93;	1920,	23·80	
Lower Chindwin	...	...	27·18;	1920,	18·14	
Upper Chindwin	...	...	55·48			
Sagaing	...	...	... 32·14			
Shwebo	...	...	... 38·08;	1920,	23·64	
Mandalay	...	...	31·57			
Katha	...	...	... 51·70;	1920,	36·81	
Bhamo	...	...	... 68·77			

Myitkyina ...	...	...	80·05
Taung-gyi ...	...	...	61·96
Tiddim ...	...	...	59·99
Sandoway ...	...	...	232·86
Kyaukpyu...	...	...	192·05
Akyab ...	...	...	253·13
Paletwa ...	...	...	138·74; 1920, 104·85

APPENDIX II

ADMINISTRATIVE DIVISIONS

(See p. 111)

The rearrangement of Divisions is as follows:

Division	Head-quarters	Districts
Upper Burma		
N.E. Frontier Division	Mandalay	Bhamo, Myitkyina, Putao, Shan States
Mandalay	Mandalay	Mandalay, Kyauksè, Myingyan, Meiktila, Yamèthin, Minbu, Magwe
N.W. Frontier Division	Sagaing	Sagaing, Upper Chindwin, Lower Chindwin, Shwebo, Chin Hills, Katha, Pakôkku [Pakôkku Chin Hills]
Lower Burma		
Arakan	Akyab	Akyab, Hill District of Arakan, Kyaukpyu, Sandoway
Irrawaddy	Bassein	Bassein, Myaungmya, Henzada, Maubin, Pyapôn
Rangoon	Rangoon	Rangoon, Hanthawaddy, Insein
Pegu	Rangoon	Pegu, Tharrawaddy, Prome, Thayetmyo, Toungoo
Tenasserim	Moulmein	Amherst, Thatôn, Salween, Tavoy, Mergui

Commissioners have been or are to be relieved of their judicial functions, except that the Commissioner will still be Sessions Judge for the Hill District of Arakan, Kyankpyu, Sandoway, Myitkyina, Putao, and Bhamo.

Similarly Deputy Commissioners will cease to be District Judges except in the last mentioned districts and in the Upper Chindwin. The Divisional and Sessions Judge of Amherst will be Sessions Judge in Salween.

APPENDIX III

LIST OF THE SHAN AND KARENNI STATES

(See pp. 115–17)

(1)

Northern Shan States

Name of State	Area in square miles*	Population*
Hsipaw (Thibaw)	4,400	122,129
Manglün (Mainglin)	2,800	40,000
North Hsenwi (Theinni)	6,335	201,175
South Hsenwi (Theinni)	2,281	85,110
Tawngpeng (Taungbaing) ...	778	31,976
Möng Mit (Momeik)	3,562	53,214

(2)

Southern Shan States

	Area	Population
Hopöng (Hopôn)	212	13,153
Hsa-tūng (Thatôn)	471	11,453
Hsa Möng Hkām (Thamakan) ...	293	15,509
Kehsi-Mānsām (Kyethi Bansan)	497	18,393
Kēnglün (Kyainglin)	54	5,291
Kēngtūng (Kyaingtôn)	12,400	200,344
Kyawkku (Kyaukku)	76	4,636
Kyong (Kyôn)	24	2,577
Lai Hka (Lègya)	1,560	30,947
Lawksawk (Yatsauk)	2,362	28,970
Loi Ai (Lwe È)	156	5,939
Loi Löng (Lwèlôn)	1,084	39,498
Loimaw (Lwèmaw)	48	5,045
Maw (Baw)	741	8,262
Mawkmai (Maukmè)	2,200	31,892
Mawnāng (Bawnin)	39	4,644
Möng Hsu (Maingshu)	470	20,913
Möng Küng (Maingkaing) ...	1,593	35,222
Möng Nai (Monè)	2,904	47,848
Möng Nawng (Maingnaung) ...	1,646	42,538
Möng Pai (Mobyè)	730	20,287
Möng Pan (Maingpan)	2,988	18,554
Möng Pawn (Maingpun)	366	15,145
Möng Sit (Maingseik)	357	7,838
Namhkök (Nankôk)	108	6,920
Namtôk (Nantôk)	14	910
Nawng Wawn (Naungmun) ...	28	4,143
Pangmi (Pinhmi)	30	3,529

* These figures are approximate.

Name of State			Area in square miles*	Population*
Pāngtāra (Pindaya)	...	...	86	16,789
Pwèla (Pwehla)	...	...	102	8,835
Sākôi (Sagwe)	...	...	82	2,162
Samkā (Saga)	...	...	314	15,742
Wanyin (Banyin) ...	...	...	219	11,254
Yawnghwe (Nyaungywe)...	...	1,302	111,557
Ye Ngan (Ywangan)	...	...	359	10,107

(3)

Under Commissioner, North West Frontier Division
Singaling Hkamti (Zingalein Kanti)
Hsawnghsup (Thaungthut)

(4)

Under Commissioner, North East Frontier Division
Hkamti Lŏng (Kantigyi)

(5)

Karenni States

Bawlakè	...	...	...	...	500	8,649
Kantarawadi (Eastern Karenni) ...					3,000	39,198
Kyèbogyi	...	...	...	...	700	12,785
Nawng Palai (Naungpalè)...			...		30	1,153

APPENDIX IV

ADMINISTRATION OF THE SHAN STATES

(See p. 115)

The Federation of the Northern and Southern Shan States took effect from 1 October, 1922. The Federation consists of the Northern and Southern Shan States set forth in Appendix III, together with the towns of Taung-gyi, Loilem, and Kalaw. One object is understood to be the removal of the Shan States from the jurisdiction of the Legislative Body of Burma.

The States will be under the general control of the Commissioner, North Eastern Frontier Division. There will still be a Superintendent at Taung-gyi and one at Lashio.

* Approximate.

An Advisory Council of Chiefs, constituted to discuss matters of general interest to the States will consist of ten Chiefs of the Southern and five of the Northern States, with four representatives of minor Chiefs of the Southern States. The Commissioner and Superintendents will be members of this Council which will not have any legislative powers.

The Federation will be financed by contributions from individual States, by rents from the Government of Burma, by revenue from forests and mineral royalties, and will assume responsibility for certain expenditure.

APPENDIX V
TRADE AND COMMERCE
(See p. 155)

Statistics of trade for the year 1921–22 were not available till these pages were passing through the press. They do not materially affect the statements in the text. A few points may be noted.

There was a substantial decline in imports and more than an equivalent rise in exports which were valued at nearly £65,000,000. Imports of woollen, silk, and cotton goods continued to fall; and only 318 motor cars were imported from abroad, mostly from America.

Somewhat less rice was exported but the value rose to £37,000,000. The export of wolfram almost ceased.

The British Empire maintained its position as contributing the greater part of the imports, though the actual value decreased. Though still the best customer, it absorbed a somewhat smaller percentage of the exports.

German trade continued to expand; though the value of the imports was less. The decrease in the import of salt from Germany was specially marked. But she took exported goods from Rangoon to the value of £3,290,000, an enormous increase over the figure of the preceding year. No less than 217,000 tons of rice, valued at £3,750,000 went to Germany from all ports. This is a surprising fact, especially when it is noted that in the five years before the War, the average annual export of rice to that country amounted to 326,000 tons valued at £3,110,000.

Eighteen German vessels came to Rangoon.

GLOSSARY

Ahmudan, office bearer; soldier.
Atumashi, incomparable.

Bilu, demon.
Bobabaing, ancestral land.
Bohozin, drum beaten to tell the hours at Mandalay Palace.
Byit, fringe made of dani leaves.
Byôn, ruby earth.

Chinthe, a fabulous beast.

Da, knife, sword
Dayè, hog deer.
Duwa, Kachin village headman.

Einshemin, heir apparent to the throne.

Gaing-dauk, assistant to a Gaing-ôk.
Gaing-ôk, head of a group of monasteries.
Gyi, (1) great; (2) barking deer.

Hlut-daw, council chamber.
Hnget-mintha, prince bird.

Kaba-kya, rock jumper (?)
Kala, western foreigner.
Kalaga, curtain.
Kazin, low mound between fields.
Kha, river (Kachin).
Kheddah, enclosure into which wild elephants are enticed.
Kôndan, ridge of slightly elevated land in alluvial tract.
Kumlao, (village) without a headman (Kachin).
Kumsa, (village) with a headman (Kachin).
Kun, betel-nut.
Kyaung, monastery.
Kyaung-myin, horse-cat.

Lèdaw, State land.

Letpet, pickled tea.

Min, king, lord.
Mi-yata, railway train.
Mwe-bwe, Russell's viper.
Myit, river (Burmese).
Myo, city, town, township, circle (Upper Burma).
Myo-ôk, township officer.
Myosa, ruler (lit. eater) of a *myo*; Shan chief of the second rank.

Nan, river (Shan).
Nats, intermediate spirits.
Ngapi, fish paste.
Ngayè, hell.
Ngwe kun hmu, Shan chief of the third rank.

Paddy, unhusked rice.
Parabark, a black substance used in lieu of writing paper.
Paso, a man's skirt.
Paya, (1) Lord; (2) pagoda.
Paya-taga, pagoda builder.
Pôngyi, a Buddhist monk.
Pwè, a theatrical performance; also other assemblies, such as a pony race, a durbar.
Pyathat, a terraced spire.
Pyogin, nursery of rice seedlings.

Salwè, chain.
Sat, sambar.
Saung, Kachin shawl or bed-spread.
Sawbwa, Shan chief of first rank.
Shwe, golden.

Tagundaing, post adorned with streamers.
Taik, circle.
Tamein, a woman's skirt.
Taung, hill.
Taung ya, hill cultivation.
Taw-myin, jungle horse.
Taw-seik, jungle goat.

Thamadi, assessor of thathameda.

Thamin, brow-antlered deer.

Thathameda, a graduated income-tax.

Thathanabaing, head of Buddhist hierarchy.

Thein, Buddhist ordination hall.

Thugyi, headman.

Ti, umbrella; the crown of a pagoda.

Twinsa, owner (lit. eater) of a well.

Wa, Buddhist Lent.

Win, enclosure, compound.

Yoma, lit. backbone; mountain ranges in Pegu and Arakan.

Zayat, rest-house.

Zerbadi, Mahomedan-Burmese.

INDEX

www.ingramcontent.com/pod-product-compliance
Ingram Content Group UK Ltd.
Pitfield, Milton Keynes, MK11 3LW, UK
UKHW042142280225
455719UK00001B/46